B & T
2/13/84
10.95

SELF-DETERMINATION

AN ANTHOLOGY OF PHILOSOPHY AND POETRY

SELF-DETERMINATION

An Anthology of Philosophy and Poetry

Edited by

Jorn K. Bramann

Adler Publishing Company
Rochester, New York

SELF-DETERMINATION

An Anthology of Philosophy and Poetry

FIRST EDITION

all rights reserved

Copyright © 1984 by Jorn K. Bramann

No part of this book may be used or reproduced in any manner whatsoever without written permission except in the case of brief quotations embodied in critical articles or reviews.

For information address
Adler Publishing Company
P.O. Box 9342
Rochester, N.Y. 14604

ISBN 0-913623-00-8

Library of Congress Catalog Card No. 83-72046

Printed in the United States of America

This book is dedicated in admiration to those in Guatemala and the other Central American republics, who are fighting for their self-determination.

TABLE OF CONTENTS

INTRODUCTION

I. THE IDEA OF THE MODERN SELF — 25
René Descartes: *Meditations 1* and *2* — 26
Johann W. Goethe: "Prometheus" — 37

II. THE SELF AS THE AUTONOMY OF REASON — 41
Immanuel Kant: "What Is Enlightenment?" — 42
Samuel T. Coleridge: "On the Prospect of Establishing a Pantisocracy in America", and "France, an Ode", Part 2 — 51

III. SELF AND SEX — 55
Mary Wollstonecraft: from *The Rights Of Women* — 56
Emily Dickinson: "She Rose To His Requirement" — 66
Friedrich Hölderlin: "The Oaktrees" — 67

IV. THE SELF AS THE MASTER OF NATURE — 71
Johann G. Fichte: from *The Vocation Of The Scholar* — 72
William Morris: "No Master" — 80

V. THE INDEPENDENT SELF — 83
Alexis de Tocqueville: from *Democracy In America* — 84
Johann W. Goethe: "To the United States" — 91
James M. Whitfield: "America" — 92
Ralph W. Emerson: "Give All To Love" — 95

VI. THE SELF AS AGENT OF WORLD HISTORY — 101
Georg W. F. Hegel: from *The Phenomenology of the Spirit* — 102
Philip Freneau: "On Mr. Paine's *Rights Of Man*" — 109
Lord Byron: "When A Man Hath No Freedom To Fight For At Home" — 111

Self Determination

VII.	**THE SELF AS THE MAKER OF THE HUMAN WORLD**	113
	Karl Marx: from *Economic and Philosophical Manuscripts of 1844*	114
	Percy B. Shelley: "Song to the Men of England"	124
	Heinrich Heine: "The Silesian Weavers"	126
VIII.	**THE SELF AS THE HIGHER HUMAN FACULTIES**	129
	John S. Mill: from *Utilitarianism*	130
	Anonymous: Satirical Poem from *Punch*	137
	Charles Baudelaire: "The Ideal"	139
IX.	**THE SELF AS NOTHING**	143
	Fyodor Dostoyevsky: from *Notes From Underground*	144
	Matthew Arnold: "Dover Beach"	151
	Emily Dickinson: "I Heard a Fly Buzz"	153
X.	**THE SELF AS BODY**	157
	Friedrich Nietzsche: from *Thus Spoke Zarathustra*	158
	Charles Baudelaire: "Giantess"	164
	Walt Whitman: "I Sing the Body Electric"	165
XI.	**THE SELF AS AWARENESS**	169
	Henry D. Thoreau: from *Walden*	170
	William Wordsworth: "The World Is Too Much With Us"	203
	Angelus Silesius: "You Are Your Own Prison"	204
	Walt Whitman: "One's Self I Sing"	204
XII.	**THE SELF AS FLUX**	207
	Ralph W. Emerson: from "Self-Reliance"	208
	Walt Whitman: "O Living Always, Always Dying"	225
	Friedrich Nietzsche: "Ecce Homo"	226
	Johann W. Goethe: "Blissful Yearning"	226
	Arthur Rimbaud: "The Drunken Ship"	228
	APPENDIX: ILLUSTRATION NOTES	233

INTRODUCTION

The major purpose of this book is to determine the meaning of the concept of "self," and to clarify such related notions as "self-determination," "being one's self," "self-realization," "finding an identity," "authentic existence" — as well as the negation of such terms, such as "loss of self" or "self-estrangement." In the attempts to become clear about one's own life, in discussions of the ideals of a human existence, or in the analysis of social systems the above terms are often used, although their meaning is not always clear. The study of this book should enable the reader to discern with some ease what is at stake when people discuss such things as "finding myself," "identity crisis," or "alienation." It should provide precision, depth, and orientation to the thoughts of those who have begun to inquire into the basic priorities of their lives.

A second purpose is to survey the historical development of the concept of self as it has emerged in the past prior to the twentieth century. What was considered finding one's self two hundred years ago is not the same as it is now. The collected reading should convey a sense of how the idea of self has shifted from emphasizing certain features in the human personality to emphasizing others. The survey is, to be sure, far from complete. But it should be sufficient to show how contemporary notions of self have evolved from their historical predecessors.

A third purpose of the book is to document the variety of self-conceptions which are available today. There are those that emphasize the faculty of reason, those that emphasize body and instincts, and those that oppose any definition of the self altogether. The comparison of these differing conceptions of self should enable the reader to see more clearly what a certain definition of self amounts to, and what consequences it has for the life of a person who defines his or her self in a certain way.

In spite of the considerable variety of self-conceptions presented here, however, there is a common notion running through all of them. It is the notion that in modern times a genuine self can emerge only through a process of emancipation, of extricating the self from a number of involvements which are seen as external to the self, and which are likely to prevent a person from truly being himself or herself. The real self, in other words, is not simply the person as we encounter him or her in ordinary situations, but is more or less hidden under social roles, deceptive physical appearances, or misleading pronouncements. A short survey of the philosophical authors presented here will elucidate this point.

(1) The idea of the modern, emancipated self was conceived most forcefully by René Descartes — which is one of the reasons why he is known as "the father of modern philosophy." Descartes wrote about defining the self at a time of vast and profound social changes, namely during the final dissolution of the medieval world. This vanishing world was characterized by a social order which had lasted for centuries, and which had offered for every individual a pre-determined position in a fixed hierarchy. People were Christians, peasants, subjects of certain lords, and/or members of similar communities, and such memberships determined their station in life, their roles, privileges, obligations, and expectations. If such questions as the purpose of one's life came up at all, they could be answered with relative ease in terms of the basic orientations of the given communities. The medieval world was a stable world in which the problem of personal identity hardly arose, where the question "who am I?" did not make much sense.

During Descartes' lifetime this stable world had fallen apart. Large numbers of peasant serfs had fled the countryside to build new lives in the growing urban centers; the cities had grown in wealth to a point where they could successfully challenge the privileges and the political power of the traditional feudal lords; innumerable new professions came into being as a result of dramatic breakthroughs in science and technology; whole new empires were created by the discovery and annexation of overseas territories;

ideological shifts and uncertainties became prominent because of the division of Western Christianity into a multitude of churches and sects. It was a time of turmoil and instability, and it created the possibility or necessity for numerous uprooted individuals to find new positions, roles, values, and identities. Traditions which survived were not felt to be reliable anymore; people became increasingly used to questioning all authority and customary wisdom. For intellectuals it was a time of deep scepticism and numerous attempts to find new beginnings. Thus, Descartes starts out his *Meditations* with a program of radical doubt, and a search for a new basis of knowledge and self-understanding:

"It is some time ago since I perceived that, from my earliest years, I have received many false opinions as true, and that what I have since based on such unstable principles could not but be very doubtful and uncertain; and ever since, I have realized that I would have to undertake seriously once in my life to be rid of all the opinions I had previously received into my credence, and start all over again from the foundations, if I wanted to establish something firm and constant in the sciences."

The secure basis of science which Descartes found in his meditations was his own reason, his pure power of thought – unadulterated by traditional teachings, the pressure of other scientists, the influence of feelings, or even the assumptions of common sense. The one stable point in an unstable world, in other words, was one's own rationality, the intellect. And it was at the same time the answer to the questions "Who am I?," "What is my real self?" My proper self was not, as common sense might assume, my whole person with all its physical, emotional, and mental aspects, let alone its role in the community, but solely the isolated thinking part of me. "I think, therefore I am" – with these words Descartes declared that my identity was independent of whether I am man or woman, black or white, Muslim or Jew, Swedish or Malaysian, a teacher or an engineer, or whatever other form my existence may take. The only thing which defines myself is reason, the fact that I think. Thinking is the inner center of my being, and to be true to myself means to emancipate myself as much as possible from the above non-rational features of my life.

(The preceding remarks are not to deny that there were forerunners of Descartes' view. The tendency to identify the real self with the soul or the mind, as opposed to the body and its "base" instincts and passions, is as old as Western philosophy. The thought of Plato, and most of Christian theology, are prominent examples. Nobody, however, was as radical and explicit as Descartes in identifying the self with thinking.)

(2) Immanuel Kant is in agreement with Descartes in defining the self as reason. And as in Descartes' image of man, the rational core of human nature is thought to be independent of and, ideally, in control of, the body and the emotions. But as many other eighteenth century Enlightenment philosophers, Kant saw reason not only in opposition to the non-rational aspects of the individual, but also to the unreasonable social conditions of the world. Descartes, afraid of the Inquisition which had just condemned Galileo for teaching that the earth traveled around the sun, was anxious to deny any revolutionary implications of his program of radical doubt; he declared his whole enterprise a strictly individual one. But Kant, in line with the entire Enlightenment movement, aimed at political reforms. A world which was governed by absolute monarchs, superstitions, and unenlightened traditions had to be changed to comply with the demands of reason. While Kant himself had no opportunity to become involved in practical political activities, he saw some of his ideals realized by the revolutions which brought about the American and French republics.

Rational self-determination is at the heart of Kant's philosophy; to be one's self is to follow the guidance of one's own reason. Thus he wrote in his essay "What is Enlightenment?":

"Enlightenment is the release of human beings from their self-incurred tutelage. Tutelage is the inability to use one's reason without direction from someone else. This tutelage is self-incurred when its cause does not lie in the lack of reason, but in the lack of resolution and courage to use it without direction from someone else. *Sapere aude!* Have courage to use your own reason! — this is the motto of enlightenment."

Kant suggests a close analogy between becoming enlightened and growing up. It is natural for a child to be taken care of, and to be guided by parents or other guardians. Childhood implies dependency. Growing up, by contrast, implies becoming able and willing to take care of oneself, and becoming responsible for one's life. It is obvious, however, that many people are physically adults, while mentally remaining dependent on all kinds of authorities and institutions that serve as substitute parents. Instead of thinking and acting themselves, they are content to accept whatever is decided for them. It is such an "escape from freedom" (as Erich Fromm called it) against which most of Kant's moral philosophy is directed. In the area of morality, *e.g.*, people are not to passively follow existing customs and moral rules, but to actively examine the rationality of any demand and any prohibition. By the same token, in the area of law and government, citizens are not to accept obediently and uncritically whatever is handed down by the authorities, but rather to examine every decree, and to resist it if it is incompatible with reason. And with respect to any tradition, enlightened people cannot consider anything sacred simply because it has existed for a long time; acceptable is only that which can be shown to be rational here and now. Whatever is accepted from authorities or from the past is to be accepted on one's own responsibility; nowhere can an adult person make himself or herself morally dependent on unexamined institutions. Enlightenment is incompatible with passive trust and blind faith.

To be one's self, then, requires a high degree of independence from most of the external conditions which control most people's lives, from powers that be, social pressures, established ways of life, as well as the urges of the body or the inclinations of the soul. The Kantian rational self emerges by emancipating itself from everything which is not rational. A person's true self is the unabridged autonomy of reason.

(3) Mary Wollstonecraft was thoroughly committed to the principles of the Enlightenment, and that brought her into sharp conflict with a civilization which had deeply internalized the dominance of males. The Enlightenment taught that all human beings are basically equal in that they are all rational beings, and that such traits as a person's race, sex, religion, or national origin are of secondary, if not negligible importance. Yet, humanity was stubbornly divided by such differences—often enough by even those individuals who professed to follow the principles of the Enlightenment. Generally, women were treated as if they were a different kind of being, a kind that needed a different upbringing and treatment than men. In the practice of most societies, women were treated as if their sex were a primary, and their rationality a secondary feature.

Throughout her book, *The Rights of Women*, Wollstonecraft complains about the fact that women are expected and trained to be obedient, submissive, gentle, frail, innocent, fair, and other things considered properly "feminine." She points out that by such demands men make women either into childish playthings for their masters' pleasure, or into creatures who get what they need by cunning because they cannot exercise their autonomy openly. The cult of "femininity" deforms the human nature of women: " . . . and while (women) have been stripped of the virtues that should clothe humanity, they have been decked with artificial graces that enable them to exercise a short-lived tyranny. Love, in their bosoms, taking the place of every nobler passion, their sole ambition is to be fair, to raise emotions instead of inspiring respect; and this ignoble desire, like the servility in absolute monarchies, destroys all strength of character" (*The Rights of Women*, Chapter II).

Women, by being "feminine," are alienated from their true selves. Their "femininity" is not a self-expression, but a mask which they are encouraged to wear. If men were to live with them as they really are, they would have to recognize them as equals, *i.e.*, as primarily rational beings. Which would imply that they themselves had to shed their roles of masters and guardians in favor of being what they basically are, namely also just rational beings: "I love man as my fellow; but his sceptre, real or usurped, extends not to me, unless the reason of an individual demands my hommage; and even then the submission is to reason, and not to man" (*ibid.*).

(4) Johann G. Fichte was a Kantian, although both philosophically and politically more openly radical than his teacher. He followed Kant in defining the self as reason, and in postulating that both the social world and one's own body and soul should be ruled by rational principles. He placed somewhat more explicit emphasis on the goal of rational, human control of nature. In fact, his whole view of reality was one of the opposition of two basic forces: the rational self and non-rational nature (the latter including body, emotions, and the entire physical world). He defined as the purpose of a human life the constant expansion of rational control over everything natural: "To subject everything that is not rational, to rule it freely and according to his own laws – that is the ultimate purpose of man" (*The Vocation of the Scholar*). Fichte realized, of course, that nature will never be entirely controlled by humanity, and that people will never be able to eliminate all traits of unreasonableness from their own behavior. But to strive, through constantly improving technology and ever extended education and self-discipline, for the continuing enlargement of the human (as opposed to natural) realm – that was his vision of self-determination.

Fichte's statements concerning the subjection of nature contain more than a tinge of a will to power. It should be underlined, therefore, that this drive for control was rigidly checked with respect to other human beings. Fichte had little feeling for the independent worth of nature, but he was a determined republican. The control over nature was to be achieved by an egalitarian, democratically administered society. Monarchies and other forms of minority rule he considered irrational and anachronistic: "The [social] drive aims at finding free, rational beings outside of ourselves, and at forming a community with them. It does not aim at subordination, as would be the case in the physical realm, but at coordination" (*ibid.*). To be one's self, in other words, requires that one rule *over* nature, but be *with* other human beings, respecting them as rational beings as much as one respects one's self. To be one's self implies being social in this sense.

(5) The American Revolution of 1776 and the French Revolution of 1789 were the most visible expressions of the aspirations of the Enlightenment, and the two events provoked a flood of conservative and progressive commentaries. The idea of a society without powerful rulers, established aristocracies, and structuring traditions intrigued the intellectuals of the time profoundly. Alexis de Tocqueville, a conservative politician at the time when the French Revolution had already been largely undone, traveled in the United States to study the legal system of a republic. The result was his *Democracy in America*, in which he described the character of a people that tried to live without many of the traditional institutions of the Old World. About "the philosophical method of the Americans" he writes: "To evade the bondage of system and habits, of family maxims, class-opinions, and, to some degree, of national prejudices; to accept tradition only as a means of information, and existing facts only as a lesson used in doing otherwise and doing better; to seek the reasons of things for oneself, and in oneself alone; to tend to results without being bound to means, and to aim at the substance through the form; — such are the principle characteristics of what I shall call the philosophical method of the Americans." From statements such as these it becomes clear why the United States was considered at the time as much more than just another country. America was seen as the land where people could live and develop without all the traditional restrictions and limitations of the Old World, where people were at liberty to create themselves out of their own visions and resources. America was the present and the future; it was the land of the Enlightenment. In it humanity could develop a degree of self-determination which it had never reached before. It was in every respect a New World.

(6) Georg W. F. Hegel, by contrast, can be characterized as a philosopher whose major energy was directed toward making life within the institutions and traditions of the Old World meaningful. What unites Hegel

with the other thinkers in this book is the realization that a conscious modern self cannot naively identify anymore with its external roles in society, or its inherited cultural values. The course of Western history had effected too deep a cut between the individual consciousness and its external environment for such naive identifications. Hegel emphasizes, *e.g.*, the role of Christianity, particularly in its Protestant form, in severing the individual's loyalties to all worldly institutions and communities by establishing a direct and overriding relationship between the person and a universal God. A person who is primarily responsible to God can only have conditional and tentative commitments to such things as nation, profession, or family. Hegel, in other words, conceives of the modern self in a very similar way as Descartes, namely as a fundamentally solitary being that only secondarily establishes relationships to the world. But after having reached this conception, Hegel then proceeds to reconstitute, as it were, the validity of all the external institutions and traditions from which the modern self was cut off. His final conclusion is that an individual has to align itself with the external forces by which it finds itself surrounded, *i.e.*, to make itself the conscious agent of the powers which make up the dialectical drama of actual history.

The reason for this recommended commitment lies in Hegel's conviction that only the real movements of history carry any philosophical weight, while the mere thoughts and ideals of individuals, no matter how wise, are without significance. The ultimate sense of world history, according to Hegel, does not lie in the thoughts of people, but in the facts themselves. Thus, a person who is serious about self-realization will align himself or herself with the historical powers that be – not naively, but on the basis of an understanding of world history. To be one's self is to be part of a nation, a state, a particular culture, a family, and so forth. A self without such affiliations is a nothing.

Hegel's emphasis on actual historical forces and institutions is primarily responsible for his reputation as a conservative "Prussian State Philosopher." For while the Prussian police were hunting down anti-monarchistic subversives, Hegel wrote in his *Outline of The Philosophy of*

Law (1821): "Thus, this treatise . . . is nothing else than the attempt to comprehend and describe the State as something which is in itself reasonable. As a philosophical work it definitely has to stay clear of trying to construct the State as it ought to be. If it is to teach anything, it is not to tell the State how it ought to be, but how it, as a moral universe, can be understood." While many of his contemporaries considered the Prussian monarchy a sad anachronism, Hegel seemed to recommend himself to the authorities by suggesting that this state was an embodiment of reason, and that self-realization consisted in finding one's proper place in it.

(7) The special conditions of the United States (a huge territory inhabited by a very small population) permitted or forced people to place a great emphasis on individual self-reliance. Thomas Jefferson, the outstanding Enlightenment thinker of the United States, envisaged a republic of farmers who all owned enough land to be economically, and thus politically, independent. In Europe, conditions were entirely different, not only because of its traditions, and the further development of the Enlightenment had to take different forms. Natural resources were scarcer, the population much larger, and the rapidly developing shift from agricultural to industrial production created a high degree of urbanization and economic dependence of people on each other. The notions of self and self-determination, therefore, had to put considerably more emphasis on social cooperation than in the United States. In the densely populated countries of Europe, American-style individualism was literally out of place.

In analyzing the necessary preconditions for self-determination, Karl Marx fastened on the fact that the developing industrialization rapidly replaced the natural world with an entirely man-made world, and that this man-made environment was fast growing into gigantic, and sometimes threatening, dimensions. Armies of workers built huge cities, turned rivers into canals, mountains into mines, wildernesses into raw material sources, and quaint old historical landscapes into dirty, noisy, but highly productive industrial centers. The increasing rate of scientific discoveries and technological inventions seemed to make the vision of the total control of nature by man a reality. Yet, the people living in the midst of this development were as powerless as they had ever been. Without understanding the causes and the direction of events, they experienced an unprecedented population explosion, constantly over-crowded cities, the uprooting of whole cultures, the vanishing of old professions and ways of life, vast economic booms and collapses with their gluts and shortages, complex and impersonal bureaucracies, and finally the beginnings of mechanized warfare which brought degrees of destruction that had never been seen before. In the huge and crowded living silos where most of the population began to live, people experienced deep loneliness and anxiety. They began to feel like strangers in the industrial landscape which they had created. The phenomenon of the Alienation of Modern Man began to emerge.

Marx analyzed the alienation and powerlessness of people, and he indicated the conditions under which this situation could be changed. The heart of the matter for Marx is work. Most people have to work for a living, and they spend the better part of their lives on the job. Yet, under modern capitalistic conditions, most people do not own the machines, the raw materials, nor the energy which are needed for production, *i.e.*, they have to work for someone else. As a result they have little or no real control over the work process in which they are involved; they have to do what others tell them. This means that during the most significant part of their lives people have no control over themselves, over their own activity. They are obliged to be the obedient tools in the hands of some management (whose decisions are equally narrowly prescribed), or the mindless appendices of machines. As workers they have lost the kind of self-determination which, according to Marx' Enlightenment conviction, they should enjoy as human beings. As workers, people are reduced to the level of harnessed animals—with the simultaneous effect of reducing them in their free time as well:

"As a result, therefore, man (the worker) only feels himself freely active in his animal functions—eating, drinking, procreating, or at most in his dwelling and in dressing-up, etc.; and in his human functions [*i.e.*, in his productive activity] he no longer feels himself to be anything but an animal"(*Economic and Philosophical Manuscript of 1844*).

Not controlling the process of work is paralleled by not controlling the product. The majority of people are involved in creating the man-made environment which replaces nature, but they do not partake in its ownership, and thus in its use. What they create assumes a life of its own—often threatening their well-being. They build the chemical factories, and then suffer from the pollution of their water; they build the cars, then suffer from congested and unhealthy cities; they build the arms, then are ravaged by bombs and gas; they produce a surplus of goods, then suffer from a depressed market. Instead of enhancing the quality of their lives, they become victimized by the product of their labor. Instead of being masters of their fate, people are helplessly moved about by the forces they create: " . . . the more the worker spends himself, the more powerful becomes the alien world of objects which he creates over and against himself, the poorer he himself—his inner world—becomes, the less belongs to him as his own . . . The worker puts his life into the object; but now his life no longer belongs to him but to the object" (*ibid.*).

To terminate this alienation, to become his and her own self, workers have to assume control over the process and the product of their work. Only when they themselves can determine how they spend their working day, and how much and for what purpose they produce, will they gain their full humanity. Until then they will be nothing but the passive pawns in a game which they do not even understand, and which becomes ever more dangerous for all involved.

(8) Mill, although sometimes leaning toward socialist ideas, was a Liberal. He is, however, in agreement with Marx as far as the gratification of basic human needs are concerned. Neither for him nor for Marx is any form of self-realization possible without a certain degree of material well-being. Both thinkers agree, furthermore, that material gratification is

only one part of the fulfillment of human needs, that the specific constitution of human beings requires the gratification of the "higher" needs as well. Since both philosophers have been repeatedly accused of catering to the "lower" instincts of people, it is important to clarify their real conceptions of self-realization. Mill in particular was very explicit about the specific nature of human self-realization and happiness.

Mill, as a Utilitarian, believed "that pleasure and freedom from pain are the only things desirable as ends" (*Utilitarianism*, Chapter II). Contrary to certain prejudices, this does not reduce people to the level of animals, because "human beings have faculties more elevated than the animal appetites and, when once made conscious of them, do not regard anything as happiness which does not include their gratification" (*ibid.*). Human self-realization can be described, then, only in terms of the development and exercise of all the faculties which distinguish humans from lower animals, such as language, complex thinking, aesthetic sense, self-control, and so forth. To become one's self requires that one be emancipated from merely instinctive reactions, uncontrolled urges, and all other forms of automatic, thoughtless behaviour. If one prefers to describe human beings as animals, it is important to remember that they are of a peculiar kind, that they are animals that are capable of high degrees of refinement. A person who neglects these potentials of refinement will fall short of becoming himself or herself.

(9) Marx as a materialist gives considerably more weight to body and emotions than Kant or Fichte, but he continued the tradition of the Enlightenment by using the ideal of rational self-determination as the norm by which the life of people can be measured. He also shared the optimism of the Enlightenment as he thought it likely that people would eventually emancipate themselves from the uncontrolled process of production which produced ever greater problems. He thought it possible that the forces of nature could be harnessed for human purposes, and that society could be organized in such a way that everyone's needs are fulfilled. For Marx the modern world held great promise for humanity.

The extreme opposite vision of the modern world is harbored by the anti-hero of Fyodor Dostoyevsky's *Notes From Underground*. This nameless protagonist is a product of the Enlightenment culture like Marx: he is not a part of any traditional community; he lives, in fact, in extreme isolation in the anonymity of a big, modern city. He does not feel bound by any values, customs, or conventions, and he is free to create the purpose of his life out of his own resources. But for him this freedom is like a nightmare, for all he finds in himself is an abyss of loneliness, pain, confusion, and emptiness. With all external points of orientation and definitions gone, he finds that the remaining self is nothing but a chaos of conflicting impulses and ideas. The self as a center of his personality does not exist.

A good deal of the Underground Man's reflections consist of diatribes against reason: "I will admit that reason is a good thing. No argument about that. But reason is only reason, and it satisfies man's rational needs only . . . I, for instance, instinctively want to live, to exercise all the aspects of life in me and not only reason, which amounts to perhaps one-twentieth of the whole" (*Notes From Underground*, I, 8). Such a passage could be taken to indicate a commitment to another definition of self, such as the self as body (as in some of Nietzsche's reflections), or the self as instincts (as in Emerson's "Self-Reliance"). The belittling of reason could be seen as part of the Romantic reaction against the rationalism of the Enlightenment. But that would be a misunderstanding; the Underground Man makes no such commitment. He is at pains to show that his life and convictions are governed exactly by the principle of non-commitment. Neither reason, nor the passions, nor anything else represent the true self. The only truth about human nature is whim: "So one's own free, unrestrained choice, one's own whim, be it the wildest, one's own fancy, sometimes worked up to a frenzy—that is the most advantageous advantage that cannot be fitted into any table or scale and that causes every system and every theory to crumble into dust on contact" (*ibid.*, I, 7). To be one's self, in other words, is being anything or nothing. It does not make any difference whether one be this or that. Any form of existence is equally authentic or inauthentic. In the modern world, there is no center left, neither in the world, nor in oneself. The self is nothing.

(10) The dominant way of defining the self in Western thought was spiritualistic, *i.e.*, the self was mostly defined as spirit, mind, soul, or some such more or less non-physical entity. The writings of Plato, Christian theologians, Descartes, and Kant are prime examples. This definition was usually accompanied by an often fierce degradation of everything physical, instinctive, or in other ways close to the animal world. Sexuality in particular was considered base, and to be suppressed as much as possible. The deformations, miseries, and perversions created by this suppression have provoked sharp criticisms of the spiritualistic definition of the self. Nietzsche was one of the most passionate critics of this tradition. While pillorying the whole basic orientation of Western civilization since Socrates and Plato as wrong-headed, he offered his own defiant definition of self in *Thus Spoke Zarathustra*: "But the adult, the knowledgeable says: I am body through and through, and nothing beside it; and the soul is nothing but a word for something belonging to the body."

My true self is my body. To define myself as reason in the way Descartes or Kant did is a fundamental delusion, a vanity of intellectuals. Nietzsche does not deny that there is thinking, but for him this is only one of the functions of the body, the mind just one of its many organs. The much more comprehensive and deeper center of my existence is the awsome complexity of the organism that I am, with all its impulses, instincts, and the unfathomable depth of what Freud was to call the Unconscious. To be myself would be to give myself over to the apparent vagueries of this powerful organism, rather than trying to dominate and suppress it through the comparatively shallow mind. A life lived thusly through the mind is self-alienation.

(11) Henry D. Thoreau does not offer an explicit, philosophical definition of the self, but his detailed analysis and critique of everyday life leads to a clear notion of what he considers an authentic existence, a self that is free of all false identifications. This self can be described as a state of

vibrant awareness. It can develop when one gives up the preoccupations which have come to be considered as normal in Western civilization: excessive work, excessive material consumption, and the unending accumulation of properties. These preoccupations are characterized by Thoreau as distractions from more genuine human activities, such as the refined exercise of one's intelligence, imagination, and emotional capabilities. Thoreau's analyses are centered around the notion of living from one's inner center out, of keeping one's inner potentials alive and active, instead of allowing them to become numbed, dulled, dormant, atrophied, or in other ways deadened. Most people, due to the prevailing patterns of Western culture, are encouraged to live from the outside in, or to occupy themselves with externals altogether. They are guided by mindless traditions, fashions, customs, routines, or the expectations of others—not to mention such things as coveted social positions, ideological hypes, or prestigious institutions. They invest themselves in external roles and activities, while their human potential remains stagnant and underdeveloped. They are, in Thoreau's image, like beggars living in splendid palaces. And although they may be vaguely aware of their loss, they usually continue with their lives of "quiet desperation." Their attachment to externals is too strong to allow them to find their way back to themselves.

It is often assumed that the point of Thoreau's experiment of living in the woods at Walden Pond was to escape from society and civilization. But Thoreau was neither a loner, nor opposed to culture, and he warned the readers who wanted to change their lives not to imitate the externals of his particular life. The real point of his experiment was to explore what an unadulterated, unalienated and intensive human life might consist of: "I went to the woods because I wished to live deliberately, to front only the essential facts of life, and to see if I could not learn what it had to teach, and not, when I came to die, discover that I had not lived. I did not wish to live what was not life, living is so dear; nor did I wish to practice resignation, unless it was quite necessary. I wanted to live deep and suck out all the marrow of life, . . . " (*Walden*, "Where I Lived and What I Lived For"). That Thoreau went to the solitude of Walden Pond was largely due to the fact that all he could usually get in the society of his contemporaries was small talk, and that the activities which were considered culture hardly deserved that name. Thoreau withdrew because he did not want to be distracted by such shallow preoccupations.

It is important to notice that Thoreau (as Marx) does not define the self in terms of only one aspect of the human personality, such as reason, body, or the passions. A fully developed person will not abrogate any of these sides of human nature. The center of one's aware life may very well shift from one aspect to another, and often a complex interplay of all these aspects may be involved in one's best perceptions and activities. The real self is a state of being, rather than any particular entity.

(12) Ralph W. Emerson understood himself as a Kantian. Unlike Kant and Fichte, however, he did not think that the innermost center of a person was reason, but rather instinct or intuition: "What is the aboriginal Self, on which a universal reliance may be grounded? . . . The inquiry leads us to that source, at once the essence of genius, of virtue, and of life, which we call spontaneity or instinct. We denote this primary wisdom as intuition, whilst all later teachings are tuitions. In that deep force, the last fact behind which analysis cannot go, all things find their common origin" ("Self-Reliance"). The German Idealists considered adherence to immutable principles, and to rigidly logical deductions from them, as an expression of the true human self. Emerson considers this rather as a super-imposition on the true self, and belief in the disciplining realm of reason an illusion. Emerson recommends listening carefully to the nuances of one's feelings and following the changing flow of the emotions. This is why he defends the inconsistencies of non-rational behavior as truer than adherence to rules and positions once taken: "A foolish consistency is the hobgoblin of little minds, adored by statesmen and philosophers and diviners. With consistency a great soul has simply nothing to do" (*ibid.*). One's true self changes, in other words; an immutable self as envisaged by Kant is a fiction. The self changes as one's feelings change, and to be one's self is to

resist the temptation to arrest the flow by declaring any one state into permanence. The self is constant flux — as the world at large. This is the discovery which the quest for the self will reveal.

Emerson is a Kantian, however, in that he recommends adhering to inner intuitions rather than outside pressures. As Kant was concerned with establishing one's self's independence from such things as non-representational governments, arbitrary laws, unenlightened traditions, or religious dogmatism, Emerson warns of such encroachments on the self's autonomy as social conformity, thoughtless loyalty to parties, sects, or ideologies, and the passive adoration of cultural authorities or celebrities of the past. Like Kant, he strongly advocates a high degree of individual self-reliance: "It is easy in the world to live after the world's opinion, it is easy in solitude to live after our own; but the great man is he who in the midst of the crowd keeps with perfect sweetness the independence of solitude" (*ibid.*).

It is evident that the notion of self which runs through most of the above definitions is diametrically opposed to another one which has also played a role in the history of philosophy and in people's imagination. Many people think of realizing themselves, of finding an identity, on the model of finding a clearly delineated role in an established social context. Success in life is defined in terms of the capability of acting out such a role. And not finding such a role is experienced as a lack, a state of being lost, as a failure in becoming a full-fledged person. A person without a prescribed role may literally feel like someone who has been left out of a play. Thus, finding a role often becomes the object of a desperate search, and available roles are accepted even in the face of grave doubts about their validity, — even if accepting them means hiding many of one's actual needs and aspirations.

Usually such roles are found by turning to the past. The ways of life of the past, and their external expressions in building styles or other areas of culture, are seen as a repository of stability and security, and thus as a relief from one's own lack of self-confidence, worth, and initiative. And the attachment to the accoutrements of the past are maintained in spite of the fact that the latter are often blatantly contradicted by actual historical developments. Thus, architects have built in full earnestness such curiosities as modern city halls with Renaissance facades, institutions of mass education in the style of medieval cathedrals, banks in the form of Greek temples, and factories which look like Egyptian or Cambodian sanctuaries. The imagination of such designers dwelled in the past, although they were handling materials and were building for people that had come out of and undergone the profound changes brought about by the Industrial Revolution. The external manifestations of the past are so alluring to conservative minds not because of mere aesthetics (for appreciating genuinely old buildings is something other than imitating them), but because they seemingly hide the flow of time which is experienced with a tinge of dread. For insecure people the present is empty, and the unknown future a threat, thus they try to surround themselves with the signs of a world which apparently is immune from change. (In architecture this attitude may be harmless enough, as the only results are aesthetic curiosities. But the matter becomes deadly serious when one considers cases where military men have at their disposal the most modern means of mass destruction, while mentally living in a world where soldiering was, relatively speaking, a jolly affair. Inestimable misery has been created in this century by generals and politicians who literally did not realize in what kind of world they were living—and this does not even include the mentality of those decision makers who talk about an atomic attack as if it were nothing but a charge of the Light Brigade.)

Finding one's self according to most of the philosophers discussed in this volume, by contrast, is essentially characterized by living in the present, and by the use of the past not as a model for imitation, but "as a lesson used in doing otherwise." To live in the present implies the serious recognition of change, of the inevitable flow of time. It implies that people be flexible, alert, and ready to create their lives anew at every moment, instead of seeking a hold and security in past accomplishments. Consequently, the theme of time and change plays an important part in the writing of the above philosophers and it is intimately connected with the problem of self-determination. In Kant's essay, *e.g.*, there is an emphatic reminder that no generation has a right to establish immutable rules and dogmas for future generations (a reminder which is paralleled by Thomas Jefferson's remark that each generation of Americans ought to have the right to rewrite the Constitution). Fichte stresses that a genuine human life should be an unending process of growth and transformation; Marx' thinking is thoroughly historical in that it assumes that absolutely nothing human will ever be exempt from change; for Emerson and Thoreau the greatest dangers to living are ossified structures, habits, and routines; Nietzsche celebrates unreserved self-consumation; and so forth.

All these philosophers have an important affinity to a philosophy of time the earliest formulation of which is attributed to Heraclitus of Ephesus (c. 600 B.C.), and which is usually summarized in the statement "everything is in constant flux." When Heraclitus says that "you cannot step into the same river twice," then he expresses in a picture that a genuine human life can only be lived in the present, and that the attempt to get a hold of one's self by clinging to what seemingly does not change is based on an illusion and bound to miss true self-realization. Heraclitus' philosophy of time foreshadows what became a fundamental motivating force in the work of most of the thinkers presented here, be it Kant, Hegel, Thoreau, or Marx: the desire to find life in its purest and most intensive form, undiluted by routines, dogmas, institutions, systems, traditions, or other deadening structures, namely in the active and ever moving present. It is a philosophy which has sometimes been summarized in the mystic notion of timelessness. Emerson, *e.g.*, wrote: "[Man] cannot be happy and strong until he too lives with nature in the present, above time" ("Self-Reliance"). A well lived life is timeless in that it finds itself always in the present, never away from where the living takes place. And a realized self is never the accumulated past, and never something that persists without change. The self is the present activity of living.

The philosophers who have this affinity to Heraclitus are not always entirely consistent in their work. Fichte's idea of an immutable self, *e.g.*, goes against the spirit of Heraclitus' concept of constant flux. Wollstonecraft's downgrading of the passions of love, Kant's and Hegel's fascination with well-ordered conceptual systems, Thoreau's unquestioning adoration of the classics of antiquity, and similar phenomena may also be incompatible with the idea of living in the present. Yet, the overall orientation and significance of the work of these thinkers lies in their emphasis on movement, change, and present, and in seeing the self in the center of this kind of timelessness.

One remark about the relation of individual orientations and social relations: The emphasis in this book on such "individualistic" thinkers as Emerson and Thoreau may give the impression that the concept of self-determination developed here is something like a "personal philosophy," an expression of an attitude toward life which individuals may or may not accept, without affecting the rest of society. With a spurious kind of tolerance, readers may say that what Thoreau, for example, says, is fine for him, but that others need not bother with it if they are not so inclined. Such a reading of the following philosophical texts is, however, not only a questionable evasion of serious challenges, but also implies a thorough misunderstanding of "individualistic" philosphers. For when Emerson argues for the importance of immediacy and intensity in one's life, then he is not just venting his personal preferences, but investigating the foundations of *a social* philosophy. A society that fails to *live* in his sense, will tend to develop forms of substitute lives, such as the excessive concern with the accumulation of objects, private property, distinction through rank in rigid hierarchies, etc., and thus to become a certain kind of collective. Or when Thoreau polemicizes against excessive material production and consumptuion, while recommending contemplation and awaresess, he indirectly comments on a society which has staked its welfare on limitless economic growth, with all its hazards for environment and human psyche. The deep concern of these "individualistic" philosophers with self-development, in other words, is as much social as, *e.g.*, Marx' reflections. (Thoreau's observations about work do, in fact, coincide with and complement those of Marx.) If there is a serious challenge to a certain way of life in the analyses of Marx, then there is also one in the works of Emerson and Thoreau. Which means that their pronouncements do not fall within the realm of opinion, which people can choose according to taste or inclination, but rather within the range of claims which are either true or false, and which have to be dealt with in an objective manner.

*

It has been said that a good picture can replace twenty or more pages of prose text. Something similar can be said about a good poem. This is the main reason why the present volume contains a good deal of poetry. The poems document the fact that the ideas which inspired the philosophical texts were active in other areas of Western Culture as well, that they are part of a general consciousness which has given form to the life of our civilization. It is hoped that the included poems will illustrate and elucidate the thoughts of the philosophical texts, and that, in turn, the philosophical texts will make visible and understandable aspects of the poems which otherwise may have remained in the dark.

During the last decades, which have been dominated by the literary ideas of the New Criticism, poems have largely been understood as aesthetic compositions, rather than historical, biographical, sociological or ideological documents. "A poem should not mean / but be," as Archibald MacLeish put it. While this was a beneficial corrective in literary criticism in view of the former neglect of aesthetic autonomy, it has by now become somewhat stale, and has induced readers to overlook such things as the philosophical or political implications of a poem. Poems, after all, can mean a great deal, and poets are often very much intent on getting a point across. This recent overemphasis may excuse, then, the somewhat one-sided, but hopefully not obnoxious philosophical use which is made of poetry in this book.

All translations are by the editor, unless indicated otherwise. I sincerely thank James Hadra, Robert Kramer and John Moran for their translations, Joy Kroger Mappes for her advice, and Arthur R. Axelrod for his very valuable help.

Finzel, Maryland
Spring, 1983

1. Nature and Geometry

I. The Idea Of The Modern Self

Self Determination

René Descartes: *Meditations* 1 and 2

AUTHOR AND TEXT: *René Descartes (1596-1650), after completing his formal education in France, spent many years traveling and soldiering in several countries. Basically, however, he was a scholar, and he kept close contact with the scientific developments of the time. In 1633 he was about to publish a scientific treatise called* The World, *when he heard of Galileo's condemnation by the the Inquisition. Since Descartes subscribed, like Galileo, to the then heretical view that the earth travels around the sun, and since he did not want to make the then powerful Catholic Church his enemy, he prevented the publication of his book. In 1637 he published his* Discourse On Method, *in which he developed a program of radical doubt of all acquired teachings and opinions—a doubt which he intended to be the beginning of an absolutely indubitable, scientific knowledge. This program, too, raised the suspicions of Church authorities, and in 1641 Descartes published his* Meditation, *in which he further defended his program of radical doubt, but in which he also tried to show that this program would not necessarily be in conflict with the doctrines of the Church. The present selection represents the entire first, and the first half of the second Meditation, in which Descartes explains his program of radical doubt. The translation is by John Moran.*

DESCARTES' RADICAL DOUBT AND ITS RELATION TO THE DEFINITION OF 'SELF': *Descartes lived at a time when scholars and other intellectuals were still trying to come to terms with the body of knowledge and opinion which they had inherited from the Middle Ages. Obviously, many of these opinions did not hold up in the light of the rapidly developing natural sciences; the heritage had to be sifted to separate truth from falsehood. While many scholars argued for a piecemeal process of revision, Descartes distinguished himself by trying to solve the problem in one fell swoop. His idea was to discard not only that which was proven false, leaving very much that was doubtful, but to discard everything which can be doubted at all. By retaining only that which would withstand even the most radical doubt, one would have something from which, by* *a rigid and scientific procedure, further insights could be deduced, thus building a reliable body of scientific knowledge.*

The question arises: is there anything which cannot possibly be doubted? One can, of course, doubt such things as specific teachings in such fields as medicine or history; there is nothing especially radical in doing so. Descartes, however, extended his doubt to the existence of the entire external world in assuming that the world which I see around me may be as illusory as a madman's hallucinations. As I can never be sure whether I am hallucinating (dreaming) or not, I should even discard my conviction that I have this body, this mind, or that I exist at all. All this can be doubted. But—and here comes the end of doubt—when I doubt that I think, then I am doubting. And if I doubt that I doubt, then I am still doubting. And if I doubt that, then I only confirm what I try to deny. In short, I cannot transcend my doubting by doubt, and this, then, will be the starting point, the foundation, of all certain knowledge. Doubting is thinking, and thinking implies the existence of a thinker. I exist insofar as I think. My existence as a thinking being, then, is the basis on which the future body of scientific knowledge is to be built. Not nature, but my mind is what can be known with the highest degree of immediate certainty.

This also answers the question of who I am, of what my innermost self consists of: I am a "thinking substance," or the act of thinking. I am identical with my mind—a mind which only secondarily inhabits a body.

SOME PRACTICAL IMPLICATIONS OF DESCARTES' THEORY: *By defining the innermost nature of human beings as mind, Descartes furthers the ideal of the rule of mind over the body, and over nature in general. Mind is superior, nature is inferior; mind is the master, nature the slave. And wherever nature rebels against the value of the mind, it has to be subdued by force.*

In the Western tradition mind is often characterized by logical order, by mathematical regularity. This is strikingly expressed in the predominant architecture of the age of Descartes. In his Discourse, *Descartes writes: "Thus it is observable that the buildings which a single architect has planned and executed, are generally more elegant and commodious than those which several have attempted to improve, by making old walls serve for purposes for which they were not originally built. Thus also, those ancient cities which, from being at first only villages, have become, in course of time, large towns, are usually but ill laid out compared with the regularly constructed towns which a professional architect has freely planned on an open plain; so that although the several buildings of the former may often equal or surpass in beauty those of the latter, yet when one observes their indiscriminate juxtaposition, there a large one and here a small, and the consequent crookedness and irregularity of the streets, one is disposed to allege that chance rather than any human will guided by reason must have led to such an arrangement."* It is clear that Descartes is thinking of such architecture as the castle, park, and town of Versailles, where the symmetrical design of one architectural will was superimposed on nature and historically grown communities, and where trees and bushes were trimmed in the shapes of cones, spheres and cubes.

The dominance of the rational mind over nature can easily turn into a kind of rape, particularly if one thinks of the inner nature, the soul. Certain moral systems, e.g., have been excessively repressive, often cruelly subduing everything which has to do with body, sexuality, fantasy, and irrational longings (sometimes provoking romantic rebellions against this kind of rationalism, which also found their expression in architecture and literature). Awareness of the supressed, non-rational nature in people has prompted many philosophers to deny the superiority of the rational mind, and to define the innermost nature of human beings in terms of emotions, intuitions, and instincts. (This is, e.g., Emerson's position in "Self-Reliance.") The rule of the logical mind, according to these philosophers, is a falsification and perversion of human nature rather than an expression of it, and the task of finding one's real self consists largely in the attempt to deflate and undercut the pretensions of the rational mind.

~ ~ ~

I have not just now learned that, from my earliest years, I have received many false opinions as true, and that what I have since based on such unstable principles could not but be very doubtful and uncertain; and ever since, I have realized that I would have to undertake seriously once in my life to be rid of all the opinions I had previously received into my credence, and start all over again from the foundations, if I wanted to establish something firm and constant in the sciences. But this seemed to me to be a very large undertaking and I waited until I reached such a ripe age that I could not hope for a later time when I would be better suited to carry it out; which has made me postpone it for so long that already I believe I would be making a mistake if I still used in deliberations the time remaining to me to act. So today, quite opportunely for this plan, I have freed my mind of all sorts of cares; fortunately feeling undisturbed by any passions, and having found a secure repose in peaceful solitude, I shall apply myself seriously and freely to the general destruction of all my old opinions. Now, to this end, it will not be necessary for me to show that they are all false, a task which I might never be able to finish. But because reason already persuades me that I should no less carefully avoid credence to things which are not entirely certain and indubitable, than to those which seem to me to be manifestly false, it will suffice for me to reject them all if I can find in each some reason to doubt. And for that too there will be no need for me to examine each of them in particular, which would be an endless task. But because the destruction of the foundation necessarily takes with it all the rest of the edifice, I shall first attack the principles by which all my old opinions were supported.

All that I have hitherto received as the most true and assured, I have from the senses or by the senses. Now, I have sometimes found that these senses are deceptive; and it is wise never to rely entirely on those who have deceived us once.

But it may be that, while the senses sometimes deceive us about things that are hardly perceptible and very far away, nonetheless many other things are encountered which cannot reasonably be doubted although we know them by means of the senses: for example, that I am here, sitting by the fire, wearing a dressing gown, having this paper in my hands, and other things of this nature. And how could I deny that these hands and this body are mine, unless I am compared with certain madmen whose brains are so disturbed and obfuscated by the black bile vapors that they continually maintain that they are kings when they are very poor; that they are clothed in gold and purple when they are naked; or who imagine themselves to be cruets or to have a glass body. But they are mad and I would be no less extravagant than they if I followed their example.

Here, however, I must take into account that I am a man and consequently that I am accustomed to sleeping and representing in my dreams the same things these madmen do when they are awake, and sometimes less plausible things. How often it has happened that I dreamed at night that I was by the fire, though I was quite naked in my bed! It seems to me at present that it is not at all with sleepy eyes that I am looking at this paper; that this head I am shaking is not nodding at all; that it is with intent and deliberate purpose that I extend this hand and sense it. What happens in sleep seems nowhere nearly as clear and distinct as all this. But, thinking about it carefully, I am reminded of having been deceived by similar illusions while sleeping; and, lingering on this thought, I see so clearly that there is no certain index at all by which wakefulness can be clearly distinguished from sleep, that I am quite amazed and my amazement is such that it is almost capable of persuading me that I am sleeping.

So now let us suppose that we are asleep and that all these particulars, namely that our eyes are open, that we are shaking our head, that we are extending our hands, and similar things, are merely false illusions; and let us think that neither our hands nor our whole body are as we see them. However, we must at least avow that the things represented to us in sleep are like a tableau or a painting. which can be formed only as a likeness of something real and genuine; and so, at least these general things, namely eyes, a head, hands and a whole body, are not imaginary but real and existent. For in truth, painters, even when they try with the greatest artifice to represent sirens and satyrs by bizarre and extraordinary figures, are nonetheless incapable of giving them entirely novel forms and natures, but only make a certain blend and composition of the parts of various animals; or even if their imagination is extravagant enough to invent something so new that nothing like it has ever been seen, and thus their work is an entirely fake and absolutely false thing, certainly at the very least, the colors from which they compose them must be real. And, for the same reason, even if these general things, namely a body, eyes, a head, hands and other similar things, could be imaginary, still we must necessarily avow that there are at least some others even simpler and more universal that are true and existent; from the mixture of which, neither more than nor less than that of some veritable colors are formed, all these images of things which reside in our thought—be they true and real, be they fake and fantastic.

Belonging to this class of things is corporeal nature in general and its extension; including the figure of extended things, their quantity or size, and their number; as well as the place where they are, the time that measures their duration and other such. That is why we might not conclude badly from that if we say that physics, astronomy, medicine and all the other sciences that depend upon the consideration of composite things are very dubious and uncertain while arithmetic, geometry and the other sciences of this nature, which treat only of very simple and very general things, without much concern for whether or not they exist in nature, contain something certain and indubitable: for, whether I am awake or sleeping, two and three joined together will always form the number five; and the square will never have more than four sides; and it does not seem possible that truths so clear and so apparent can be suspected of any falsity or uncertainty.

However, I have long had in my mind a certain opinion that there is a God who can do anything, and by whom I have been made and created as I am. But, how do I know that what He has brought about is that there is neither earth nor sky nor extended body nor figure nor size nor place and that nevertheless I have impressions of all these things, and that it all seems to me not to exist other than as I see it.

And even as I sometimes think that others are mistaken in the things they think they know best, how do I know that He has not brought about that I too am mistaken every time I add two and three, or when I count the sides of a square, or when I judge of something even easier, if anything easier is imaginable? But perhaps God did not will that I should be deceived in that way, for He is said to be supremely good. However, if it was repugnant to His goodness to have made me so that I was always mistaken, it would also seem to be inconsistent for Him to permit me to be sometimes mistaken; and nevertheless I cannot doubt that He permits it. At this point there might be some persons who would prefer to deny the existence of such a powerful God than to believe that all the other things are uncertain. But let us not resist them for the present, and in their favor let us suppose everything said here about a God to be a fable. Nonetheless, in whatever way they suppose I have come to my present state of being, whether they attribute it to some destiny or fate, whether they refer it to chance, whether they want it to be by a continual sequence and linking of things or by any other way; since to err and be mistaken is an imperfection, however less powerful the author to whom they attribute my origin may be, so much more probable will it be that I am so imperfect that I am always mistaken. To these reasonings I surely have no response but am at last constrained to avow that there is nothing of all that I formerly believed to be true which I cannot in some way doubt, and that not for thoughtlessness or levity but for very strong and maturely considered reasons. So henceforth I should no less carefully refrain from giving credence here than to what is manifestly false if I want to find something certain and assured in the sciences.

But it does not suffice to have made these observations. I must take care to remember them: for these old and ordinary opinions still recur frequently in my thought. the long familiarity they have had with me giving them the right to occupy my mind against my will, becoming almost masters of my credence; and I shall never break the habit of deferring to them and trusting in them so long as I consider them such as indeed they are, which is to say in some way doubtful, as I have just shown, and nonetheless very probable, so that there is much more reason to believe them than to deny them. That is why I think I shall not do badly if, in deliberately taking a contrary view, I deceive myself and pretend for some time that all these opinions are entirely false and imaginary; until at last, having so balanced my old and my new prejudices that they cannot tilt my mind more to one side than the other, my judgment will no longer be controlled by bad practices and stray from the right path that might lead it to knowledge of the truth. For I am confident that there is neither danger nor error on this path and that I am incapable of according too much to my distrust at the present since it is not now a question of acting but only of meditating and knowing.

Thus I shall suppose not that God, who is very good and who is the supreme source of truth, but that a certain evil genie, no less cunning and deceitful than powerful, has employed all his industry to deceive me; I shall assume that the sky, the air, the earth, colors, shapes, sounds and all other external things are just illusions and dreams which he has used to lay traps for my credulity; I shall consider myself to have no hands, no eyes, no flesh, no blood, as not having any senses yet falsely believing that I have all these things. I shall stubbornly abide by this thought; and if, by this method, it is not within my power to come to knowledge of any truth, at the very least it is in my power to suspend my judgment. That is why I shall prepare my mind so well against all the ruses of this great deceiver that, powerful and cunning as he may be, he will never be able to impose anything on me.

But this project is painful and laborious, and a certain indolence draws me imperceptibly into the path of my ordinary life. Just as a slave who enjoys an imaginary liberty in his sleep, when he begins to suspect that his liberty is only a dream, is afraid to wake up and conspires with his pleasant illusions to be further seduced by them, so I slip back imperceptibly into my old opinions, and I am apprehensive about waking from this drowsiness for fear that the laborious vigil which would succeed the tranquility of this repose, instead of bringing me some daylight in the knowledge of the truth, will be insufficient to dispel all the darkness of the difficulties that have just been raised.

*

Yesterdays's meditation has filled my mind with so many doubts that it is no longer in my power to forget them. And I still do not see how I shall be able to resolve them; as if I were thrown suddenly into deep water, I am so disconcerted that I can neither plant my feet on the bottom nor swim to keep afloat on the surface. Nevertheless I shall exert myself to follow again the same path on which I started yesterday, discarding everything in which I can imagine the least doubt just as if I knew it is absolutely false. And I shall continue in this way until I have found something certain or at least if I cannot do anything else, until I have grasped with certainty that nothing in the world is certain. Archimedes, in order to move the terrestrial globe from one place to another, asked only for one fixed and immovable point; thus I shall be entitled to entertain high hopes if I am fortunate enough to find only one thing that would be certain and indubitable.

Thus I suppose that all the things I see are false; I am persuaded that nothing has ever existed of all that my memory, full of falsehoods, represents to me. I consider myself to have no senses; I believe that body, figure, extension, movement and place are only fictions of my mind. What then can be considered as true? Perhaps nothing except that nothing in the world is certain.

But how do I know there is not something different from those I have just judged uncertain, of which there cannot be the least doubt? Is there not some God or some other power who puts these thoughts into my mind? That is not necessary for I might be capable of producing them myself. At the very least then, am I not something? But I hesitate, for what follows from that? Am I so dependent on the body and the senses that I cannot be without them? But I was persuaded that there was nothing at all in the world, that there were neither sky nor earth nor minds nor bodies; was I not then also persuaded that I was not at all? Far from it; without doubt, I was if I was persuaded or even if I have thought something. But there is an I-know-not-what kind of deceiver, very powerful and very cunning, who uses all his industry to deceive me. There, then, is no doubt at all that I am, if he deceives me; and let him deceive me as he will, he will never be able to turn me into nothing as long as I think I am something. So that, after having reflected on it and having carefully examined everything, it must at last be concluded and maintained that this proposition: I am, I exist, is necessarily true every time I pronounce it or conceive it in my mind.

But I, who am certain that I am, do not yet know clearly enough what I am; so that henceforth I must carefully guard against imprudently taking some other thing for me, and thus be mistaken in the knowledge I hold to be more certain and more evident than all that I previously had. That is why I shall now consider again what I thought myself to be before beginning these last reflections; and of my old opinions, I shall retrench all that can be combatted at all by the reasons I have just now advanced, so that all that remains will be precisely that alone which is entirely certain and indubitable. What then have I previously believed myself to be? Clearly, I thought I was a man. But what is a man? Shall I say that it is a rational animal? Certainly not, for then I should have to find out what an animal is, and what is rational. Thus from a single question I would gradually slip into an infinity of others even more difficult. And I do not want to waste the little time and leisure remaining to me by using it to sort out such difficulties. Instead I shall pause here to consider the thoughts that previously arose spontaneously in my mind and were inspired only by my own nature, when I applied myself to consideration of my being. I considered myself primarily as having a face, hands, arms and all that machine composed of flesh and bone, as it appears in a cadaver, and which I designate by the name of body. I further considered that I was nourished, that I walked, that I sensed and that I thought, and I attributed all these actions to the soul. But I did not stop to think what this soul was or, if I did I imagined it was something extremely rare and subtle such as a wind, a flame, or a very fine air which was insinuated and diffused throughout my coarser parts. As for what was body, I never had any doubt about its nature but thought I knew it very distinctly and if I had wanted to explain it according to the notions of it which I had at the time, I would have described it in this way: by body I mean all that which can be bounded by some figure, which can be contained in some place and occupy a space in such a way that all other bodies are excluded from it; which can be sensed either by touch or sight or hearing or taste or smell; which can be moved in various ways, not really by itself but by something alien to it by which it might be touched and from which it would receive an impulse; for, to have the power of being moved by itself, as well as feeling and thinking, I did not believe belonged to the nature of body at all; on the contrary, I was rather surprised to see that similar faculties were encountered in certain bodies.

But me, who am I, now that I suppose there is a certain genie who is extremely powerful and, if I dare to say so, malicious and cunning, who employs all his might and industry to deceive me? Can I be sure that I have anything at all of those properties which previously I have said belong to the nature of body? I pause to think attentively, I go over and over all these things in my mind and I do not find any of them of which I am able to say that it belongs to me. There is no need to stop to enumerate them. So let us go on to the attributes of the soul and let us see whether any of them would belong to me. The first are being nourished and walking, but if it is true that I have no body then it is also true that I can neither walk nor be nourished. Another is sensing, but one cannot sense without the body; besides, I have formerly thought that I sensed some things in my sleep which upon waking I recognized that I had not really sensed. Another is thinking, and I find here that thought is an attribute that belongs to me; it alone cannot be separated from me. I am, I exist, that is certain; but for how long? As long as I think. For it might happen that, if I stopped thinking altogether, I would at the same time altogether cease being. I am now admitting nothing that would not be necessarily true. Thus I am, speaking precisely, only a thinking thing; that is to say, a mind, an understanding or a reason, which are terms whose meaning was previously unknown to me. Now, I am a real thing and really existent, but what thing? I have already said it, a thing that thinks. And what more? I shall stimulate my imagination in order to see whether I am not anything more. I am not at all this assemblage of members called the human body; I am not at all a fine and penetrating air diffused through all these members; I am not at all a wind, a breath, a vapor nor any of all that I can stimulate and imagine, since I have supposed that all that was nothing and, without changing that supposition, I find I do not cease being certain that I am something.

Johann W. Goethe: "Prometheus"

Descartes' emphasis on confidence in one's own reason, as opposed to confidence in external authorities and tradition, inspired the eighteenth century Enlightenment. It also inspired, besides atheism, forms of religion in which the divine was not conceived as a powerful lord or father, but rather as a principle in nature or of morality. The very idea of external authorities had become very repugnant to Enlightenment thinkers. For this reason the Greek myth of Prometheus, the hero who stole the fire from the gods to enable humanity to become independent and able to create civilization, became part of the Enlightenment imagination. Goethe's poem "Prometheus" is an example of this anti-authoritarian defiance.

Goethe's life (1749-1832) spanned the periods of Enlightenment as well as Romanticism. "Prometheus" belongs to his early works. It is one of the earliest free verse poems in the German language.

Cover your sky, Zeus,
With clouds
And exert yourself, like a boy
Who is cutting thistles
Among oak trees and hills,
In the end you will have to leave me the earth
And my house,
Which you have not built,

And my hearth,
The fire of which you envy me.

I do not know anything more miserable
Under the sun than you, gods!
You feed your majesty poorly
With sacrifices
And the weak breath of prayers,
And you would starve, if
Children and beggars
Were not such hopeful fools.

When I was a child
And had lost my way
I turned my erring eye
Toward the sun, as if above
There were an ear to hear my complaint,
A heart like mine,
to take pity on those in need.

Who helped me
Against the attacks of the tyrants?
Who saved me from death
And slavery?
Did you not accomplish everything yourself,
Holy glowing heart?
You glowed strong and well,
Although betrayed—should I thank, then,
The sleeper above?

Honor you? For what?
Have you ever given relief
For the pain of the oppressed?
Have you ever stopped the tears
Of the terrified?
Was it not all powerful time
That has forged me into a man,
And eternal fate—
Your master as much as mine?

Did you imagine
That I should hate life
And flee into deserts
Just because not all
My dreams bore fruit?
Here I sit, forming men
After my own image —
A race equal to myself,
To suffer, to cry,
To enjoy, and to rejoice,
And to ignore you —
Like me!

2. Prometheus

II. THE SELF AS THE AUTONOMY OF REASON

SELF DETERMINATION

Immanuel Kant: "What Is Enlightenment?"

AUTHOR AND TEXT: *Immanuel Kant (1724-1804) was one of the most influential defenders of the moral and political principles of the Enlightenment. The Enlightenment was an intellectual movement which dominated the thinking of the eighteenth century, the "Age of Reason." Its essential passion was the will to judge and organize everything according to reason. Reason was to be the ultimate judge not only in matters of morals, law, and politics, but also in aesthetics and religion. By advocating the use of reason the promotors of the Enlightenment came into numerous conflicts with the established powers: they battled with orthodox theologians, with churches, and with any form of absolute political power. They used reason as a means of subversion. The American and French revolutions were in many ways the practical expressions of the philosophy of the Enlightenment.*

Kant's essay "What is Enlightenment?" was written in 1784 for a journal in Berlin. In it he defends the basic tenet of the Enlightenment, the right to use one's own reason publicly, i.e., the right of free speech. Kant's stand appears rather modest; he explicitly refrains from challenging the absolute power of the monarch under whom he lived. (A few years later, after the French revolution broke out, Kant privately sympathized with the revolutionaries, in spite of the fact that the revolution was widely denounced in Europe.) Kant's modesty in his essay was an attempt to save at least the few freedoms that existed then in Prussia. At the time these freedoms were under attack from many sides, and a few years later they were, in effect, abolished.

The prince to whom Kant refers in his essay was Frederick the Great (1712-1786), King of Prussia. Frederick was a paradoxical figure. He was, on one hand, one of the best educated and most enlightened monarchs of his time who actively promoted many of the goals of the Enlightenment. He insisted on religious tolerance, abolished torture from the legal system, and introduced significant agrarian reforms. He was fluent in French, corresponded with and was host to such eminent philosophers as Voltaire, played the flute, composed and hosted such musicians as J. S. Bach. He considered himself, and lived like, "the first servant of his state." But he deeply mistrusted people. One of his maxims was: "Everything for the people, nothing by the people." And so he was, on the other hand, a ruthlessly dictatorial ruler, who enforced discipline, particularly in the army, often by cruel means. He also waged several wars of aggression which, although successful in terms of territorial gains, impoverished Prussia and its citizens to the utmost degree. By such measures as reserving all officer's posts in the powerful army for the hereditary aristocracy, he insured that Prussia would be, as long as it existed, one of the most conservative countries in Europe.

SELF AND COMMUNITY: *Kant places a high value on personal autonomy, i.e., on the freedom of the individual to decide things for himself or herself without interference from external forces. Yet, human beings are social animals. (This does not mean that all individuals are gregarious, but it means that even the classical hermit depends on other human beings and society for language, thought, and a definition of his role.) It is important to notice that Kant's concern with personal autonomy does not blind him to the fact that people have to be part of some kind of social situation. What he argued was that society should have no irrational power over its members, that human society should be based on rational cooperation.*

KANT AND THE TWENTIETH CENTURY: *Kant is in several ways a preparer of twentieth century consciousness. By describing the mature person as an individual who relies on his or her own reason, rather than depending on the established or traditional rules, values and customs of his community, Kant foreshadows the twentieth century individual who has lost all genuine contact with communities, who suffers from isolation and disorientation because of the lack of binding norms and a common center, and who feels that his or her autonomy has turned into a state of total loss. Jean-Paul Sartre's Existentialist philosophy, e.g., is very much inspired by Kant's idea of self-determination: "Man is nothing else but that which he makes of himself. That is the first principle of Existentialism" ("Existentialism is a Humanism," 1946). This seemingly positive link between Sartre and Kant appears in a very negative light when Sartre describes the human condition further in the following way: "The Existentialist finds it extremely embarrassing that God does not exist . . . Dostoyevsky once wrote 'If God does not exist, everything would be permitted', and that, for Existentialism, is the starting point. Everything is indeed permitted if God does not exist, and man is in consequence forlorn, for he cannot find anything to depend upon either within or outside himself . . . That is what I mean when I say that man is condemned to be free"* (ibid.). *While Kant was proud of the self-reliance of the individual, and felt the intellectual independence of a person from his or her environment to be a gain, Sartre tends to describe that situation as oppressive and in need of being overcome by an arbitrary, desperate commitment to some chosen cause. Yet, the basic idea of the self as an independent agent in the world is very similar in the philosophies of both men.*

~ ~ ~

Enlightenment is the release of human beings from their self-incurred tutelage. Tutelage is the inability to use one's reason without direction from someone else. This tutelage is self-incurred when its cause does not lie in the lack of reason, but in the lack of resolution and courage to use it without direction from someone else. *Sapere Aude!* Have courage to use your own reason! — this is the motto of enlightenment.

Laziness and cowardice are the reasons why so many people, long after nature has released them from external direction, like to remain under lifelong tutelage, and why it is so easy for others to assume the roles of their guardians. It is so easy to remain a minor. If I have a book that thinks for me, a priest who has a conscience for me, a physician who decides my diet, etc., I need not make any efforts myself. I need not think myself, as long as I can pay — others will do the unpleasant work for me. That the greater part of humanity (including the entire fair sex) thinks that the step to emancipation is not only arduous, but also dangerous, is seen to by those guardians who have so kindly assumed superintendence over their lives. After they have first made their cattle dumb and have made sure that these silent creatures will not dare to move without the harness of the cart to which they are chained, the guardians then show them the danger which threatens them if they should try to move by themselves. This danger, however, is not really so great, for by falling a few times they would finally learn how to walk without aid. But an example of falling tends to make people timid, and usually frightens them away from any further trials.

Thus for every individual it is difficult to work his way out of the condition of tutelage, which has almost become a natural condition. People even like this condition, and at present they are actually incapable of using their own reason, since nobody has ever allowed them to try using it. Statutes and formulas, those mechanical devices of a rational use, or rather misuse, of our natural gifts, are the fetters of a permanent tutelage. The person who throws them off would, nevertheless, make only an uncertain leap across even the narrowest gap, for he is not used to that kind of free movement. Because of this there are only few who have both escaped tutelage through their own efforts, and also achieved a steady pace.

It is by far more possible that an entire public enlighten itself; in fact, if only freedom be granted, enlightenment is almost certain to follow. For there will always be some who think for themselves, even among the established guardians of the masses, and they will, after shaking off the yoke of tutelage from their own shoulders, spread the spirit of a reasonable appreciation of one's own worth and everybody's duty to think for one's self. It should be noted, incidentally, that the public, which has first been brought under the yoke of their guardians, often forces these leaders themselves to remain fettered when the masses are incited to do so by some other leaders who are incapable of any enlightenment—so harmful is it to implant prejudices, because they are bound to take vengeance on those who cultivated them, as well as on their descendants. Thus, a public can only slowly become enlightened. A revolution can perhaps achieve the fall of personal despotism, or some exploitative and tyrannical oppression, but never a true reform of the way people think. Rather, new prejudices will serve as well as old ones to manipulate the stupified masses.

For enlightenment, however, nothing is required but freedom — in fact, the most harmless kind among all those things that can thusly be called, namely the freedom to make public use of one's reason in every respect. But now I hear on all sides: Don't argue! The officer says: Do not argue, but drill! The taxation official: Do not argue, but pay! The cleric: Do not argue, but have faith! (Only one prince in the world says: Argue as much as you will, and about what you will, but obey!) Everywhere freedom is restricted. Which restriction, however, is an obstacle to enlightenment, and which one is not — or even a help for it? I answer: the public use of one's reason must at all times be free, and it alone can bring about enlightenment among people, while the private use of one's reason can often be restricted rather narrowly without particularly hindering the progress of enlightenment. By the public use of one's reason I understand the use which an individual makes of it as a scholar before the reading public. By private use I understand that which a person may make of it in a particular civil post or some other office. Some affairs which are conducted in the interest of the community must conform passively and with artificial unanimity, so that the government can direct them to public ends — or at least prevent them from doing damage to these ends. In such cases arguments are not permissible; one must obey. Insofar, however, as a part of this machine considers himself also as a member of a whole community, or even as a world citizen, and hence in the role of a scholar who writes for the public (in the proper meaning of this word), he certainly can argue without damaging the affairs for which he is in part responsible as a passively obeying functionary. For example, it would be ruinous for an officer on military duty to argue about the suitability or usefulness of an order given to him by his superior; he must obey. But the right to comment on mistakes of the military, and to present them to the public for their judgment cannot justifiably be denied him as a scholar. The citizen cannot refuse to pay the taxes imposed on him; in fact, an impudent criticism of such taxation can be punished as a scandal, if it could incite a general resistance. The same person, nevertheless, does not violate his duties as a citizen when he publishes his thoughts on the inappropriateness or injustice of these taxes as a scholar. In the same way a cleric is obliged to give his sermon to his pupils in catechism and his congregation in conformity with the symbol of the church which he serves, for he has been employed on this condition. As a scholar, however, he has complete freedom, even the duty, to publish all his well-meaning and carefully tested thoughts on that which may be flawed in the symbol, and to offer his proposals for the better organization of religion and church. There is nothing in this that could be a burden for his conscience. For what he teaches as a representative of the church is something about which he is not at liberty to teach according to his own reason; it is something which he is employed to disseminate at the direction of and in the name of someone else. He will say: our church teaches this and this, and these are the proofs which it adduces. He then extracts all practical uses for his congregation from statutes to which he himself may not subscribe with full conviction, but to the dissemination of which he can apply himself because it is not impossible that there is some truth in them, or that there is at least nothing in them that would contradict inner religion. For if he thought that he had found something of the sort in them, he could not serve in his office any longer with a good conscience; he would have to resign. The use, therefore, which an employed teacher makes of his reason in his congregation is only private, because his congregation, no matter how large, is necessarily a domestic one. In this respect a cleric is not free; he cannot be free, because he carries out the task of someone else. As a scholar, by contrast, whose writings are addressed to the public as such, i.e., to the world, the cleric enjoys unrestricted freedom in the use of his own reason. For that the guardians of the people in spiritual matters should themselves be under the condition of tutelage is an absurdity which is tantamount to the eternalization of absurdities.

But should not a society of clerics, such as a church or a venerable *classis* (as they are called among the Dutch), have the right to bind itself by oath to a certain unchangeable symbol to enjoy an everlasting guardianship over each of its members, and thereby over the people in general? I answer that this is entirely impossible. Such a contract, which would foreclose all further enlightenment from the human race, is absolutely null and void, even if confirmed by the supreme power, by parliaments, or by the most solemn peace treaties. No age can conspire to put the following one under such a condition that it cannot extend its knowledge, correct errors, and progress toward general enlightenment. That would be a crime against human nature, the original destination of which is precisely this kind of progress. Future ages would be entirely justified in rejecting such decrees as having been issued in an unwarranted and malicious manner.

The touchstone of everything that can be decreed as a law for a people lies in the question: could the people have imposed such a law on itself? Now, such a religious decree may be possible for a short time, in expectation, as it were, of a better. During this time, while the law remains in effect, every citizen, and especially the cleric in the role of scholar, could make free and public comments concerning the questionable aspects of the present order, until insights into these matters have progressed to such a point, where, by uniting their voices (although not necessarily unanimously), the citizens could petition the throne to take those congregations under protection which have opted for a changed religious order in accordance with their own best understanding. Without, however, imposing on those who prefer to remain in the old order. But to agree on a permanent religious institution which is not to be subject to public doubt, and thereby to render a whole period fruitless with respect to the progress of humanity, working to the disadvantage of posterity, is, even for the lifetime of an individual, absolutely unacceptable. A person can, to be sure, postpone for a limited time his or her enlightenment. But to renounce enlightenment forever, and to renounce it on behalf of posterity, that amounts to trampling underfoot the most sacred rights of humanity. And what a people cannot decide for itself can even less be decreed for it by a monarch, for a monarch's law-giving authority rests on his representation of the general public will. If he only sees to it that all true or assumed improvements are compatible with the civil order, he can safely leave it to his subjects to do themselves what they find necessary for their spiritual welfare. To care about that does not fall within the range of his duties, though he is obliged to prevent any one of his subjects from forcefully hindering others to determine and promote their welfare to the best of their ability. A monarch would, in fact, lower his own majesty if he meddled in these matters by subjecting the publications, in which his subjects are striving for clarification, to his governmental supervision. And it does not matter whether he would do so by enunciating his own convictions, in which case he would be open to the reproach *Caesar non est supra grammaticos*, or by supporting the ecclesiastical despotism of a particular tyrant in his state against his other subjects.

If the question is raised: are we now living in an enlightened age? – the answer is: no, but in an age of enlightenment. It could hardly be maintained that people are, under the present condition, generally capable of making use of their own reason in religious matters without outside direction. But there are clear signs that the field has been opened wherein people may freely deal with these matters, and that the obstacles to general enlightenment, or to the release from self-incurred tutelage, are gradually reduced. In this sense ours is the age of enlightenment, or the century of Frederick.

A prince who does not find it unworthy of himself to declare that he takes it to be his duty to prescribe nothing to people in religious matters, but to grant them complete freedom in this area, who thereby even renounces the presumptuous title of tolerance, is himself enlightened, and deserves to be praised by a grateful world and posterity as the first who delivered humanity from tutelage at least from the side of government, and who left every person free to make use of his reason in matters of conscience. Under his government respectable clerics are allowed, in the role of scholars, and without violation of their official duties, to submit their insights and judgments, which sometimes deviate from established symbols, to public scrutiny. Even greater freedom is enjoyed by those who are not restricted by any official duties. This spirit of freedom spreads beyond the boundaries of this state into those areas where it encounters the external obstacles erected by governments which do not understand their own interest. These governments have now an example which shows that freedom is no threat to public peace and unity of commonwealth. People will work their way out of barbarism if only no artificial obstacles are erected to keep them in it.

I have put the main point of enlightenment—the release of human beings from their self-incurred tutelage—in religious matters, because our rulers have no interest in directing the arts and sciences, and also because religious tutelage is not only the most harmful, but also the most degrading lack of autonomy. But the attitude of the head of state who favors religious freedom has wider implications. Such a monarch sees that there is no danger to his legislative power when he allows his subjects to make public use of their reason, and to publish their thoughts on better formulations of his laws, or even to freely criticize the laws already made. Of such an attitude we have a shining example, and no monarch has yet been superior to him whom we honor.

Only he who is himself enlightened, who is not afraid of shadows, but who also has a large and well-disciplined army to insure public peace, can say what a republic would never dare to say: Argue as much as you will, and about what you will, but obey! Here shows itself a strange and unexpected course in human affairs, as paradoxical as most things in human history when looked at in a general way. A higher degree of civil liberty appears to further intellectual freedom, yet, it places unsurmountable limitations on it. A lower degree of civil liberty, by contrast, provides the mind with the space to allow its expansions in all directions. Once nature has developed under a hard shell the seed for which it cares most tenderly, namely the propensity and vocation to think freely, this seed will effect the principles of the government, a government which will find it appropriate to treat human beings, who will have become more than machines, according to their dignity.

Samuel T. Coleridge:

"On The Prospects Of Establishing
A Pantisocracy In America"

and

"France, an Ode," Part 2

Coleridge (1772-1834) was a versatile English Romanticist, who wrote poetry, literary criticism, and philosophical reflections. In the twentieth century he became particularly important in discussions about poetry, as his poem "Kubla Khan" was written under the influence of opium, thus foreshadowing later theories concerning the importance of the unconscious in the production of literary texts. The phases of his intellectual life were typical of the biography of so many Romantic minds: early disenchantment with his own society, hope for revolutionary changes, resigned turning away from society.

Around 1794, Coleridge and a group of friends conceived a plan to emigrate to the United States, and to found an ideal community (the "Pantisocracy" of the first poem). The poem "On the Prospect . . ." contrasts the war-torn Europe (a conservative alliance of monarchs was about to invade France to undo the revolution there, England's crown being one of the instigators) with the "content and bliss" of the New World. What is important in this context is the fact that Coleridge does not sympathize with his own country against France, but that he sympathizes with the ideals for which the French armies were fighting at the time. As mentioned before, it was one of the ideals of the Enlightenment to enable people to rise above the narrow boundaries of one's own sex, race, religion, or national origin, and to appreciate the demands of reason wherever they may be voiced.

SELF DETERMINATION

"France, An Ode" was written around 1798, when France's fight against monarchism had begun to develop new forms of tyranny. Coleridge began to lose hope in revolution as a means to achieve freedom. But the second part of the ode (reprinted here) still testifies to his Enlightenment standards, and to his alienation from his own country because of its anti-Enlightenment politics.

Whilst pale Anxiety, corrosive Care,
The tear of Woe, the gloom of sad Despair,
 And deepened Anguish generous bosoms rend; —
Whilst patriot souls their country's fate lament;
Whilst mad with rage demoniac, foul intent,
 Embattled legions Despots vainly send
To arrest the immortal mind's expanding ray
 Of everlasting Truth; — I other climes
Where dawns, with hope serene, a brighter day
 Than e'er saw Albion in her happiest times,
With mental eye exulting now explore,
 And soon with kindred minds shall haste to enjoy
(Free from the ills which here our peace destroy)
 Content and Bliss on Translantic shore.

*

When France in wrath her giant-limbs upreared,
 And with that oath, which smote air, earth, and sea,
 Stamped her strong foot and said she would be free,
Bear witness for me, how I hoped and feared!
With what a joy my lofty gratulation
 Unawed I sang, amid a slavish band:
And when to whelm the disenchanted nation,
 Like fiends embattled by a wizard's wand,
  The Monarchs marched in evil day,
  And Britain joined the dire array;
Though dear her shores and circling ocean,
Though many friendships, many youthful loves

  Had swoln the patriot emotion
And flung a magic light o'er all her hills and groves;
Yet still my voice, unaltered, sang defeat
  To all that braved the tyrant-quelling lance,
And shame too long delayed and vain retreat!
For ne'er, O Liberty! with partial aim
I dimmed thy light or damped thy holy flame;
  But blessed the paeans of delivered France,
And hung my head and wept at Britain's name.

III. Self and Sex

SELF DETERMINATION

Mary Wollstonecraft: *The Rights Of Women*

AUTHOR AND TEXT: *Mary Wollstonecraft (1759-1797; usually listed in Encyclopedias under her husband's name, Godwin) was a feminist and political radical in the circle of Thomas Paine, William Blake, William Godwin, and other anti-monarchists. The title of her book* The Rights of Women *(1792) is an obvious allusion to Paine's* Rights of Man *(which is a defense of the French Revolution of 1789 against its conservative critic Edmund Burke). In 1792 she traveled to Paris to observe the revolution, and she addressed the National Assembly there to press for the equalization of male and female education. She also published a book on the education of women. She was the mother of Mary Wollstonecraft (1797-1851), who was the nineteen year old author of* Frankenstein, or the Modern Prometheus, *and the second wife of Percy B. Shelley.*

REASON AND EMOTIONS: *Wollstonecraft is firmly committed to the rationalism of the Enlightenment. Her argument aims at recognizing women as the equals of men with respect to the most fundamental human feature: reason. In the course of her deliberations she makes some downgrading remarks about the emotional features of humans, such as the following:* "Love, the common passion, in which chance and sensation take the place of choice and reason, is, in some degree, felt by the mass of mankind; for it is not necessary to speak, at present, of the emotions that rise above or sink below love. This passion, naturally increased by suspense and difficulties, draws the mind out of its accustomed state, and exalts the affections; but the security of marriage, allowing the fever of love to subside, a healthy temperature is thought insipid only by those who have not sufficient intellect to substitute the calm tenderness of friendship, the confidence of respect, instead of blind admiration, and the sensual emotions of fondness" *(*The Rights of Women, *Chapter II).*

Such remarks raise two questions: (a) Is reason indeed the most fundamental human feature? Or is rationalism a subtle form of self-alienation, an alienation from one's deepest and most intimate roots? Many Romantics, many feminists, and authors like Emerson or Nietzsche defend the latter position. (b) Should women become incorporated into a rationalistic culture? Or should not men rather learn to be more emotional? Many argue that Western Civilization has always been excessively rational, and that reason is to blame as the fundamental cause of most of the difficulties in our culture.

In discussing these questions one can refer back to what has been remarked about Descartes' rationalism and its implications. There certainly is such a thing as suppressing body and emotions in an unhealthy, damaging way. On the other hand, it can hardly be maintained that people have tortured and burned "witches," unleashed wars of conquest and annihilation, or lived under the rule of brutal monarchs because they were all too reasonable and thoughtful. Such things as greed, fear, ignorance, and indifference are much more likely motivating forces for such historical events than rationality. The entire ongoing debate between the Rationalists and their adversaries, between Enlightenment and Romanticism, is conceptually rather confused, and thus has made both parties to the dispute the victims of questionable cliches and slogans. In fact, the traditional opposition between Reason and Emotion is itself very questionable, and stands in need of closer scrutiny.

The present excerpts are parts of the second chapter of The Rights of Women.

~ ~ ~

To account for, and excuse the tyranny of man, many ingenious arguments have been brought forward to prove, that the two sexes, in the acquirement of virtue, ought to aim at attaining a very different character; or, to speak explicitly, women are not allowed to have sufficient strength of mind to acquire what really deserves the name of virtue. Yet it should seem, allowing them to have souls, that there is but one way appointed by Providence to lead *mankind* to either virtue or happiness.

If then women are not a swarm of ephemeron triflers, why should they be kept in ignorance under the specious name of innocence? Men complain, and with reason, of the follies and caprices of our sex, when they do not keenly satirise our headstrong passions and grovelling vices. Behold, I should answer, the natural effect of ignorance! The mind will ever be unstable that has only prejudices to rest on, and the current will run with destructive fury when there are no barriers to break its force. Women are told from their infancy, and taught by the example of their mothers, that a little knowledge of human weakness, justly termed cunning, softness of temper, *outward* obedience, and a scrupulous attention to a puerile kind of propriety, will obtain for them the protection of man; and should they be beautiful, everything else is needless, for at least twenty years of their lives.

Thus Milton describes our first frail mother; though when he tells us that women are formed for softness and sweet attractive grace, I cannot comprehend his meaning, unless, in the true Mahometan strain, he meant to deprive us of souls, and insinuate that we were beings only designed by sweet attractive grace, and docile blind obedience, to gratify the senses of man when he can no longer soar on the wings of contemplation.

How grossly do they insult us who thus advise us only to render ourselves gentle, domestic brutes! For instance, the winning softness so warmly and frequently recommended, that governs by obeying. What childish expressions, and how insignificant is the being—can it be an immortal one?—who will condescend to govern by such sinister methods? "Certainly," says Lord Bacon, "man is of kin to the beasts by his body; and if he be not of kin to God by his spirit, he is a base and ignoble creature!" Men, indeed, appear to me to act in a very unphilosophical manner, when they try to secure the good conduct of women by attempting to keep them always in a state of childhood. Rousseau was more consistent when he wished to stop the progress of reason in both sexes, for if men eat of the tree of knowledge, women will come in for a taste; but, from the imperfect cultivation which their understandings now receive, they only attain a knowledge of evil.

Children, I grant, should be innocent; but when the epithet is applied to men, or women, it is but a civil term for weakness. For if it be allowed that women were destined by Providence to acquire human virtues, and, by the exercise of their understandings, that stability of character which is the firmest ground to rest our future hopes upon, they must be permitted to turn to the fountain of light, and not forced to shape their course by the twinkling of a mere satellite.

*

Women are therefore to be considered either as moral beings, or so weak that they must be entirely subjected to the superior faculties of men.

Let us examine this question. Rousseau declares that a woman should never for a moment feel herself independent, that she should be governed by fear to exercise her *natural* cunning, and made a coquettish slave in order to render her a more alluring object of desire, a *sweeter* companion to man, whenever he chooses to relax himself. He carries the arguments, which he pretends to draw from the indications of nature, still further, and insinuates that truth and fortitude, the corner-stones of all human virtue, should be cultivated with certain restrictions, because, with respect to the female character, obedience is the grand lesson which ought to be impressed with unrelenting rigour.

What nonsense! When will a great man arise with sufficient strength of mind to puff away the fumes which pride and sensuality have thus spread over the subject? If women are by nature inferior to men, their virtues must be the same in quality, if not in degree, or virtue is a relative idea; consequently their conduct should be founded on the same priniciples, and have the same aim.

Connected with man as daughters, wives, and mothers, their moral character may be estimated by their manner of fulfilling those simple duties; but the end, the grand end, of their exertions should be to unfold their own faculties, and acquire the dignity of conscious virtue. They may try to render their road pleasant; but ought never to forget, in common with man, that life yields not the felicity which can satisfy an immortal soul. I do not mean to insinuate that either sex should be so lost in abstract reflections or distant views as to forget the affections and duties that lie before them, and are, in truth, the means appointed to produce the fruit of life; on the contrary, I would warmly recommend them, even while I assert, that they afford most satisfaction when they are considered in their true sober light.

Probably the prevailing opinion that woman was created for man, may have taken its rise from Moses' poetical story; yet as very few, it is presumed, who have bestowed any serious thought on the subject ever supposed that Eve was, literally speaking, one of Adam's ribs, the deduction must be allowed to fall to the ground, or only be so far admitted as it proves that man, from the remotest antiquity, found it convenient to exert his strength to subjugate his companion, and his invention to show that she ought to have her neck bent under the yoke, because the whole creation was only created for his convenience or pleasure.

Let it not be concluded that I wish to invert the order of things. I have already granted that, from the constitution of their bodies, men seemed to be designed by Providence to attain a greater degree of virtue. I speak collectively of the whole sex; but I see not the shadow of a reason to conclude that their virtues should differ in respect to their nature. In fact, how can they, if virtue has only one eternal standard? I must therefore, if I reason consequentially, as strenuously maintain that they have the same simple direction as that there is a God.

It follows then that cunning should not be opposed to wisdom, little cares to great exertions, or insipid softness, varnished over with the name of gentleness, to that fortitude which grand views alone can inspire.

I shall be told that woman would then lose many of her peculiar graces, and the opinion of a well-known poet might be quoted to refute my unqualified assertion. For Pope has said, in the name of the whole male sex:

Yet ne'er so sure our passion to create
As when she touch'd the brink of all we hate.

In what light this sally places men and women I shall leave to the judicious to determine. Meanwhile, I shall content myself with observing, that I cannot discover why, unless they are mortal, females should always be degraded by being made subservient to love or lust.

To speak disrespectfully of love is, I know, high treason against sentiment and fine feelings; but I wish to speak the simple language of truth, and rather to address the head than the heart. To endeavour to reason love out of the world would be to out-Quixote Cervantes, and equally offend against common sense; but an endeavour to restrain this tumultuous passion, and to prove that it should not be allowed to dethrone superior powers, or to usurp the sceptre which the understanding should very coolly wield, appears less wild.

Youth is the season for love in both sexes; but in those days of thoughtless enjoyment provision should be made for the more important years of life, when reflection takes the place of sensation. But Rousseau, and most of the male writers who have followed his steps, have warmly inculcated that the whole tendency of female education ought to be directed to one point – to render them pleasing.

Let me reason with the supporters of this opinion who have any knowledge of human nature. Do they imagine that marriage can eradicate the habitude of life? The woman who has been taught to please will soon find that her charms are oblique sunbeams, and that they cannot have much effect on her husband's heart when they are seen every day, when the summer is passed and gone. Will she then have sufficient native energy to look into herself for comfort, and cultivate her dormant faculties? Or is it not more rational to expect that she will try to please other men, and, in the emotions raised by the expectation of new conquests, endeavour to forget the mortification her love or pride has received? When the husband ceases to be a lover, and the time will inevitably come, her desire of pleasing will then grow languid, or become a spring of bitterness; and love, perhaps, the most evanescent of all passions, gives place to jealousy or vanity.

I now speak of women who are restrained by principle or prejudice. Such women, though they would shrink from an intrigue with real abhorrence, yet, nevertheless, wish to be convinced by the homage of gallantry that they are cruelly neglected by their husbands; or, days and weeks are spent in dreaming of the happiness enjoyed by congenial souls, till their health is undermined and their spirits broken by discontent. How then can the great art of pleasing be such a necessary study? It is only useful to a mistress. The chaste wife and serious mother should only consider her power to please as the polish of her virtues, and the affection of her husband as one of the comforts that render her task less difficult, and her life happier. But, whether she be loved or neglected, her first wish should be to make herself respectable, and not to rely for all her happiness on a being subject to like infirmities with herself.

*

Women ought to endeavour to purify their heart; but can they do so when their uncultivated understandings make them entirely dependent on their senses for employment and amusement, when no noble pursuits set them above the little vanities of the day, or enables them to curb the wild emotions that agitate a reed, over which every passing breeze has power? To gain the affections of a virtuous man, is affectation necessary? Nature has given woman a weaker frame than man; but, to ensure her husband's affections, must a wife, who, by the exercise of her mind and body whilst she was discharging the duties of a daughter, wife, and mother, has allowed her constitution to retain its natural strength, and her nerves a healthy tone, — is she, I say, to condescend to use art, and feign a sickly delicacy, in order to secure her husband's affection? Weakness may excite tenderness, and gratify the arrogant pride of man; but the lordly caresses of a protector will not gratify a noble mind that pants for and deserves to be respected. Fondness is a poor substitute for friendship!

In a seraglio, I grant, that all these arts are necessary; the epicure must have his palate tickled, or he will sink into apathy; but have women so little ambition as to be satisfied with such a condition? Can they supinely dream life away in the lap of pleasure, or the languor of weariness, rather than assert their claim to pursue reasonable pleasures, and render themselves conspicuous by practising the virtues which dignify mankind? Surely she has not an immortal soul who can loiter life away merely employed to adorn her person, that she may amuse the languid hours, and soften the cares of a fellow-creature who is willing to be enlivened by her smiles and tricks, when the serious business of life is over.

Besides, the woman who strengthens her body and exercises her mind will, by managing her family and practising various virtues, become the friend, and not the humble dependent of her husband; and if she, by possessing such substantial qualities, merit his regard, she will not find it necessary to conceal her affection, not to pretend to an unnatural coldness of constitution to excite her husband's passions. In fact, if we revert to history, we shall find that the women who have distinguished themselves have neither been the most beautiful nor the most gentle of their sex.

*

Gentleness of manners, forbearance and long-suffering, are such amiable Godlike qualities, that in sublime poetic strains the Deity has been invested with them; and, perhaps, no representation of His goodness so strongly fastens on the human affections as those that represent Him abundant in mercy and willing to pardon. Gentleness, considered in this point of view, bears on its front all the characteristics of grandeur, combined with the winning graces of condescension; but what a different aspect it assumes when it is the submissive demeanour of dependence, the support of weakness that loves, because it wants protection; and is forbearing, because it must silently endure injuries; smiling under the lash at which it dare not snarl. Abject as this picture appears, it is the portrait of an accomplished woman, according to the received opinion of female excellence, separated by specious reasoners from human excellence. Or, they kindly restore the rib, and make one moral being of a man and woman; not forgetting to give her all the "submissive charms."

How women are to exist in that state where there is neither to be marrying nor giving in marriage, we are not told. For though moralists have agreed that the tenor of life seems to prove that *man* is prepared by various circumstances for a future state, they constantly concur in advising *woman* only to provide for the present. Gentleness, docility, and a spaniel-like affection are, on this ground, consistently recommended as the cardinal virtues of the sex; and, disregarding the arbitrary economy of nature, one writer has declared that it is masculine for a woman to be melancholy. She was created to be the toy of man, his rattle, and it must jingle in his ears whenever, dismissing reason, he chooses to be amused.

To recommend gentleness, indeed, on a broad basis is strictly philosophical. A frail being should labour to be gentle. But when forbearance confounds right and wrong, it ceases to be a virtue; and, however convenient it may be found in a companion—that companion will ever be considered as an inferior, and only inspire a vapid tenderness, which easily degenerates into contempt. Still, if advice could really make a being gentle, whose natural disposition admitted not of such a fine polish, something towards the advancement of order would be attained; but if, as might quickly be demonstrated, only affectation be produced by this indiscriminate counsel, which throws a stumbling-block in the way of gradual improvement, and true melioration of temper, the sex is not much benefited by sacrificing solid virtues to the attainment of superficial graces, though for a few years they may procure the individuals regal sway.

As a philosopher, I read with indignation the plausible epithets which men use to soften their insults; and, as a moralist, I ask what is meant by such heterogeneous associations, as fair defects, amiable weaknesses, etc.? If there be but one criterion of morals, but one archetype for man, women appear to be suspended by destiny, according to the vulgar tale of Mahomet's coffin; they have neither the unerring instinct of brutes, nor are allowed to fix the eye of reason on a perfect model. They were made to be loved, and must not aim at respect, lest they should be hunted out of society as masculine.

*

I love man as my fellow; but his sceptre, real or usurped extends not to me, unless the reason of an individual demands my homage; and even then the submission is to reason, and not to man. In fact, the conduct of an accountable being must be regulated by the operations of its own reason; or on what foundation rests the throne of God?

It appears to me necessary to dwell on these obvious truths, because females have been insulated, as it were; and while they have been stripped of the virtues that should clothe humanity, they have been decked with artificial graces that enable them to exercise a short-lived tyranny. Love, in their bosoms, taking the place of every nobler passion, their sole ambition is to be fair, to raise emotion instead of inspiring respect; and this ignoble desire, like the servility in absolute monarchies, destroys all strength of character. Liberty is the mother of virtue, and if women be, by their very constitution, slaves, and not allowed to breathe the sharp invigorating air of freedom, they must ever languish like exotics, and be reckoned beautiful flaws in nature.

As to the argument respecting the subjection in which the sex has ever been held, it retorts on man. The many have always been enthralled by the few; and monsters, who scarcely have shown any discernment of human excellence, have tyrannised over thousands of their fellow-creatures. Why have men of superior endowments submitted to such degradation? For, is it not universally acknowledged that kings, viewed collectively, have ever been inferior, in abilities and virtue, to the same number of men taken from the common mass of mankind—yet have they not, and are they not still treated with a degree of reverence that is an insult to reason? China is not the only country where a living man has been made a God. *Men* have submitted to superior strength to enjoy with impunity the pleasure of the moment; *women* have only done the same, and therefore till it is proved that the courtier, who servilely resigns the birthright of a man, is not a moral agent, it cannot be demonstrated that woman is essentially inferior to man because she has always been subjugated.

Brutal force has hitherto governed the world, and that the science of politics is in its infancy, is evident from philosophers scrupling to give the knowledge most useful to man that determinate distinction.

I shall not pursue this argument any further than to establish an obvious inference, that as sound politics diffuse liberty, mankind, including woman, will become more wise and virtuous.

Emily Dickinson: "She Rose To His Requirement"

The external life of Emily Dickinson (1830-1886) was extremely uneventful. She rarely left her native Massachusetts, she never married, and she never published a single book during her lifetime. Her writing style was not sufficiently appreciated by her contemporaries, and the depth and unusual perspectives reached in her poems were not accessible to the literary world until the twentieth century. She was another one of those writers who were half a century ahead of their time.

"She Rose to His Requirement" (1863) portrays the deep split between the outer and the inner life of a woman, the playing of a socially assigned role and the existence of a hidden, undeveloped self. The role is that of "woman and of wife," and it is honorable, according to the expectations of her husband and the world. Her real self consists of her own faculties and gifts which, if developed, would give inner wealth, breadth, and greatness to her life. But her own self is not

allowed to come out; it lies at the bottom of her soul. There, in obscurity, it creates pearls — objects which are both beautiful as well as the result of a disease. The beauty, however, is hidden from the world. Only the husband is in a position to estimate how deeply buried the hidden self of his wife really is.

> She rose to his requirement, dropped
> The playthings of her life
> To take the honorable work
> Of woman and of wife.
>
> If aught she missed in her new day
> Of amplitude, of awe,
> Or first prospective, or the gold
> In using wear away,
>
> It lay unmentioned, as the sea
> Develops pearl and weed,
> But only to himself is known
> The fathoms they abide.

Friedrich Hölderlin: "The Oaktrees"

Hölderlin (1770-1843) is best known as one of the greatest poets of classical German literature, and usually described as an unworldly Romantic. He shared, however, the ideals of the Enlightenment, and he had strong sympathies for the revolutionaries in France. In his novel Hyperion, *and in numerous poems, he analyzes, criticizes, and laments the hopelessly corrupt and ossified social conditions in Germany. Like Nietzsche, he became incurably insane during the later part of his life. His genius, like that of Dickinson, Nietzsche, Whitman or Thoreau, was not fully understood until the twentieth century.*

Self Determination

The free-verse poem "The Oaktrees" (c. 1796) evokes the contrast between nature and culture, whereby the civilized world represents everything which is weak, stunted, and docile, while free and strong development is assigned to the undomesticated wilderness. The author would give himself over to the strength and freedom of the wild, if it were not for his "hunger for love." This tie to humanity binds him to confining civilization, institutions, and domesticity. It makes him accept, against his instincts of liberty, the values of a meek society. It makes him betray his better self.

From the gardens I come to you, you sons of the mountains!
From the gardens, where nature lies domesticated and patient,
Together with industrious people, caring and cared for.
But you, glorious ones, stand like a race of Titans
In a tamed world, and you belong to yourself, and to the sky,
That has nourished you, and to the earth, that has born you.
None of you have ever gone to the schools of men,
And you push up, gaily and freely, out of strong roots,
And you grasp, like the eagle his prey,
Your space with powerful arms; and towards the clouds
Point, elated and vast, your sunbright crowns.
Each of you is a world; like the stars of the sky
You live, a god every one, in free association.
If I could only endure slavery, I would not envy
This forest, and I would embrace a life among men.
If only my heart, hungry for love, would not bind me
To life among men, how gladly would I live among you!

3. Nature and Technology

IV. THE SELF AS MASTER OF NATURE

Johann G. Fichte: The Vocation of the Scholar

AUTHOR AND TEXT: *Johann G. Fichte (1762-1814) became famous with his book* Critique of All Revelation *(1792), in which he argues in Kantian fashion that what is revealed in biblical revelations is not the existence of a divine authority above, but a moral principle within us. The success of the book among German intellectuals earned him a professorship of philosophy at the University of Jena, where he gave the lectures entitled* The Vocation of the Scholar *(1794), from which the following excerpts are taken. For a number of years Fichte was a very popular teacher, although he began to encounter certain difficulties with the authorities. During the time of his tenure the French Revolution was unfolding, and thousands of German students sympathized more or less openly with the French revolutionaries. Fichte was reported as saying in class that in a few decades the last monarchs may well vanish from Europe. Needless to say, such sentiments worried the authorities who at the time were very nervous about the possible spread of revolutionary tendencies throughout the rest of Europe. To make things worse for Fichte, he was also accused of atheism. When refusing to budge from his principles, he lost his position in 1799.*

"SELF" AND "NOT-SELF": *To understand this pair of concepts one can start with the ordinary understanding of "self": I as a person am distinguished from the world; I am that which is not the world, and the world is everything which does not belong to me as a person. In philosophy this oppositon between me and the world is maintained, but the borderline dividing the two is drawn differently. In philosophy the world does not only include that which surrounds my person, but also my body. Thus, in philosophy, my body is not, strictly speaking, part of my Self; a wedge is driven between me and my body. (This wedge was driven in the most radical way by Descartes.) My body is something alien to my Self, it is an object which can be manipulated by me in the same way as the things of the world.*

In Fichte's thought the purification of the Self of worldly things is still more radical, however. The Self, in opposing body and world, would still be a soul, an entity with feelings, instincts, fantasies, etc. But Fichte assigns not only the body, but also the soul to the world, and the remaining "Self" is nothing but pure thought. Indeed, in other writings Fichte even goes so far as to assign the process of rational thinking to the world, insofar as one can be aware of one's thoughts, thus making them an object of one's observation. In short, everything which can be made an object of my thinking is, by definition, part of the world which is opposed to my "Self." If I think of my "Self," it is not my Self anymore, because there has to be another Self that does the thinking. Thus, my real, innermost "Self" can never be an object. It exists only in the act of thinking. From this Fichte derives the conclusion that the nature of the "Self" is activity, and the nature of the "Not-Self" passivity. The "Self" is to do, and the "Not-Self" is the material of its activity.

THE DUAL NATURE OF HUMAN BEINGS: *As a pure "Self" I am a totally rational being; as an empirical person (with body and feelings) I am partly a rational, and partly a sensuous being. Fichte's general idea is that the "Self" is active, and the "Not-Self" is passive, i.e., the "Self" is to control, shape, use, or transform everything which is "Not-Self." A special case of this is that my rational nature is to subdue my sensuous (or empirical) nature. My sensuous nature is only the raw material through which my rational nature can realize itself, and in my living my life as a person I should conduct myself in such a way that my rational nature can expand itself. It is clear, however, that my rational nature needs its opposite, sensuous nature, in order to realize itself.*

"UNITY" AND "MULTIPLICITY": *The basic characteristic of the Not-Self is multiplicity, and of the Self, unity. A simple illustration of this can be provided by remembering how a person may be torn in different directions by various feelings, making him or her warm and loving in one moment, and cold or hateful the next. Such a person may be perceived as unreliable or unpredictable by others, and he or she may feel unbalanced or insecure as a consequence. Against this "multiplicity" Fichte advocates the unity of a mind that* acts and reacts according to unshakable principles, no matter what a person's momentary feelings may be.

Here is one of the most significant points of conflict with the philosophy of Emerson—in spite of their common interest in human autonomy. Emerson, as will be seen, argues against just the kind of "identity" which Fichte considers the center of a rational person.

FICHTE'S ATTITUDE TOWARD NATURE: Fichte advocates the domination of nature by a self-conscious rationality in a way which parallels the progressive replacement of the natural earth by a man-made world. His language is often drastic when he speaks of the "subjugation" of nature. This language easily evokes the contemporary scenes of bulldozers tearing through landscapes, replacing trees, grass, birds, and quiet with plastic shopping malls, parking lots, and incessant motor noise, and the connected vision of anonymous, powerful organizations pushing people around from one place to another in the interest of maximizing their gains.

Important points of Fichte's philosophy contradict this reading of his recommendations: (a) People, as rational beings, are to control nature, not destroy it. To turn swamps into gardens, e.g., need not be the reckless transformation which strip-logging is. (b) The control of nature includes not only the transformation of physical, external nature, but the humanization of the soul as well. The control of external nature by greed, drive for power, or sheer insensitivity certainly is not in Fichte's spirit. The realization of Fichte's philosophy includes the rational control and transformation of feelings or instincts of aggression, envy, and other drives which are likely to turn social life into a war of all against all. (c) In no case should people be treated as the passive objects of manipulation. The only legitimate interaction between people is cooperation based on reason.

One could possibly go a step further in an environmentalist reading of Fichte. Rational control of nature can, in many cases mean leaving nature alone. Limitless and thoughtless industrialization, e.g., hardly seems the most rational option for any population. By the same token, a *rational attitude toward one's self, one's own emotional powers, need not mean the suppression and eradication of feelings. Respecting the depth within us, listening to and enjoying the wealth of emotions, does not necessarily go against the demands of reason.*

~ ~ ~

The pure Self can only be conceived negatively, as the opposite of the Not-Self, the basic characteristics of which is multiplicity. Thus, the pure Self is conceived of as complete and absolute unity, as that which is always one and the same, and never something else. Hence the above formula can also be expressed in the following way: Man should always be identical with himself; he should never contradict his own human nature. Now, the pure Self can never contradict itself, for in it there is no diversity — it is always one and the same. But the empirical Self, which is and can be determined by external things, can very well contradict itself, and as often as it does contradict itself it indicates clearly that it is not determined by the idea of the pure Self, *i.e.*, by itself, but rather by external circumstances. This should not be, for man is his own purpose; he is to determine himself, and he should not allow himself to be determined by something alien to his inner Self. He is to be what he is because he wills it, and because he ought to will it. The empirical Self is to be shaped in such a way that it could exist in that form forever. For this reason I would formulate (in passing, and merely to illustrate) the basic principle of morality as follows: So act that you may think of the maxim of your will as an eternal law for yourself.

The ultimate vocation, then, of all finite, rational beings is absolute unity, constant identity, and complete agreement with themselves. This absolute identity is the proper form of the pure Self, and the only true form of it. Or rather: in the conceivability of this identity one recognizes the expression of this form. Whatever vocation of man can be thought of as eternally valid, that vocation would be compatible with the form of the pure Self. This, incidentally, should not be understood either partially or one-sidedly. Not the will alone should always be at one with itself (this would take care only of the area of morality), but all human faculties (which ultimately are one single power, anyway, and distinguished from each other only in their application to different problem areas) should be identical with themselves, and also accord in perfect harmony with each other.

The empirical determinations of our Self, at least the majority of them, do not depend on ourselves, but on something outside ourselves. Our will, to be sure, is absolutely free in its own circle, *i.e.*, in the area of those things to which it can be related after they have become known to us—which will be rigorously proven in due time. Our feeling however (and the intuitions emanating from it) is not free, but depends on things outside of our Self, and the nature of these things is not characterized by unity, but by multiplicity. If, in spite of this, the Self is to be at one with itself in this respect, too, it has to try to influence directly that on which depend our feelings and intuitions. Man must try to modify things and to bring them in harmony with the pure form of the Self, so that our perception of things, in so far as they depend on the nature of their objects, harmonize with this pure form. Such a modification of things according to our necessary concepts of what they ought to be is not possible by a sheer act of will, but also requires a certain dexterity which is acquired and increased with practice.

Further—and this is even more important—our empirical Self acquires itself certain deformations through the unrestricted influence of external things on it—an influence to which we open ourselves without any hesitation as long as our reason has not been fully awakened. These deformations are incompatible with the form of our pure Self, since they originate from things outside of us. For the eradication of these deformations and the regaining of the original pure form, a mere act of will is not sufficient, either. Here, too, we need the kind of dexterity that is acquired and increased by practice.

The acquisition of this dexterity to suppress and eradicate the improper inclinations which grew in us before the awakening of our reason and feeling of our own power, and to modify the things outside of us according to our own ideas—the acquisition of this dexterity, I say, is called *Culture*, and the acquired particular degree of this dexterity, is called by the same name. Culture is differentiated only by degrees, but it is capable of an infinite number of graduations. It is the last and highest means for the achievement of the ultimate goal of man, the total identity with himself—in case that man is considered as a being that is sensuous *and* rational. If man is considered merely as a sensuous being, then culture is itself the ultimate goal. For sensuousness ought to be cultured—that is the last and highest that can be done with it.

The final result of all that has been said is this: The complete identity of man with himself, and—to make this identity possible—the identity of all external things with his necessary practical concepts of them (*i.e.*, the concepts which determine what things *ought* to be)—this is the last and highest goal of human life. This identity is, to use a term of Critical Philosophy, what Kant calls the *Highest Good*—which highest good, as is clear from what has been said, does not consist of two parts, but is really one, namely the complete identity of a rational being with itself. With respect to a rational being that is dependent on external things, it is possible to consider the matter in a two-fold way; as identity of the will with the idea of an eternally valid will (*i.e.*, as moral goodness), and as identity of the things outside of us with our rational will (*i.e.*, as happiness). Thus it is, incidentally, far from true that man is motivated through his longing for happiness to strive for moral goodness. Rather, the notion of happiness itself, and the longing for it, arises out of the moral nature of man. Not that is good which produces happiness, but only that produces happiness which is good. Without morality no happiness is possible. Agreeable feelings, to be sure, are possible without morality, and even in conflict with it. (And in its proper place we will see why that is possible.) Agreeable feelings, however, are not happiness, but often even go against it.

To subject everything that is not rational, to rule it freely and according to his own laws—that is the ultimate purpose of man. This purpose is and will be in principle unattainable, as long as man is man, and not God. It is part of the concept of man that his ultimate goal be unattainable, that his way to it be infinite. It is, therefore, not the vocation of man to reach this goal. But he can and ought to come ever closer to it, and thus the unending approximation to this goal is the true vocation of all human beings, *i.e.*, the vocation of rational, but finite, free, but sensuous beings. If one calls the above identity with one's own Self perfection, perfection in the highest sense of the word, then perfection is the highest unattainable goal of man, while the unending process of perfecting himself is his vocation. He exists to become morally ever more perfect, to improve the world around him physically, and, with regard to society, morally, and to thus obtain ever greater happiness.

*

At first the social drive is characterized only negatively through the law of absolute identity with ourselves, *i.e.*, it must not contradict its own nature. The social drive aims at reciprocal activity, at mutual effects, mutual giving and receiving, mutual activity and passivity. It does not aim at mere effectivity, mere activity, which the other person would only have to suffer. The drive aims at finding free, rational beings outside of ourselves, and at forming a community with them. It does not aim at *subordination*, as would be the case in the physical realm, but at *coordination*. If one were not willing to accept other rational beings as free persons, then one would, *e.g.*, be only interested in their intellectual skills, and not in their practical, free rationality. One would not be with them in society, but one would want to dominate them as skillful animals. But in doing so one would put one's social drive in contradiction with itself. But what am I saying—putting it in contradiction with itself? In reality one does not even have it, this higher drive, humanity has not yet formed itself within us, we find ourselves still at the low level of an imperfect humanity, of slavery. We ourselves have not yet matured enough to feel our freedom and self-determination, for otherwise we would want to see around us similar, *i.e.*, free beings. We are slaves, and we want to keep slaves. Rousseau once said: "Some think of themselves as Lords over others, although they are more slaves than the latter." He could have said much more correctly: Anyone who thinks of himself as a Lord over others is himself a slave. Even if he is not a slave in reality, he surely has the soul of a slave, and he will crawl lowly before anyone who is stronger than he is, and who subjects him to his will. Only that person is free who wants to free everyone around him and who, by ways of a certain influence the cause of which has not always been recognized, makes everyone really free. Under his eyes we breathe more freely; we will not feel manipulated, repressed, or wedged in; we feel an unusual desire to be and to do everything which our self-respect does not prohibit.

Man is permitted to use objects as means for his ends, but not rational beings. He must not even use them as means to achieve their own ends. He must not effect them in the way he can effect dead matter or animals to achieve his purposes, without taking into account their own freedom. He must not make a rational being virtuous or wise or happy against his or her own will. Disregarding the fact that such an endeavor would be bound to fail, that nobody can become virtuous or wise or happy except through his or her own work and endeavor, disregarding, then, that man is incapable of doing so, nobody should, even if it were possible, even want to do so, for it is not right, and he would put himself in contradiction with himself.

Through the law of complete identity with one's Self the social drive also becomes defined positively, and thus we find the proper vocation of man in society; — all individuals that are part of the human race are different from each other. There is only one respect in which they are all the same, namely with respect to their ultimate goal, their perfection. This perfection is defined only in one way: total identity with one's Self. If all men could become perfect, if they were capable of reaching their highest and ultimate goal, then they would all be equal, they would be just one person. Now, everybody tries to raise all others up to the ideal that they have made for themselves of human beings. It follows that the highest, ultimate goal of society is the complete unity and unanimity of and among all members of it. But since reaching this goal presupposes fulfilling the vocation of man as such, the reaching of absolute perfection is as impossible as the latter—it is impossible as long as man is man, and not God. Complete unity of all individuals, then, is the ultimate goal, but not the vocation of man in society.

But to approach this goal, and to approach it without end—that man can and ought to do. The approximation of complete unity and unanimity of and among all individuals we can call unification. Thus, unification that becomes ever more intensive and extensive is the true vocation of man in society. This unification, however, is, since people agree and can agree only about the ultimate vocation of man, possible only through perfection. Thus we may as well say: Common perfection, perfection of oneself through freely used effects of others on us and through acting back on others as free beings, that is our vocation in society.

William Morris: "No Master"

One of the fundamental ideals of the Enlightenment was that people govern themselves, that they rid themselves of any lords or masters who have assumed control over their lives. At the height of the Enlightenment movement this anti-authoritarian ideal was primarily directed against political and clerical authorities, as oppression came primarily from state and church. In the nineteenth century, however, a new form of rule of men over men developed; the rule of economic power. People who control banks, industry, communications media, and natural resources also control the lives of people involved in production and consumption. And as the wealth of the big industrialists of the nineteenth century rapidly increased, their enormous power often dwarfed that of the feudal princes of the past. Economic power turned out to be in many ways more effective than mere political or doctrinal power.

As the concentration of political power in the hands of absolute monarchs finally elicited anti-monarchistic rebellions, the concentration of economic power in the hands of the owners of industry elicited the Socialist movements. While the

Enlightenment fought for political democracy, Socialists fought for social democracy. While the Enlightenment revolutionaries demanded that all political matters be decided democratically, Socialists demanded that in addition all economic matters be administered democratically. Socialists, in other words, challenged the existence of powerful masters in the same way as the Enlightenment rebels, only in a different area of life.

William Morris (1834-1896) was an English poet, craftsman, and publisher. The later part of his life was dedicated to the cause of Socialism as a way to abolish the rule of men over men. His poem "No Master" expresses the hope that one day the wage-earning masses will shed their docility and overthrow those who rule over their lives:

Saith man to man, We've heard and known
  That we no master need
To live upon this earth, or own,
  In fair and manly deed.
The grief of slaves long passed away
  For us hath forged the chain,
Till now each worker's patient day
  Builds up the House of Pain.

And we, shall we too crouch and quail,
  Ashamed, afraid of strife,
And lest our lives untimely fail
  Embrace the Death in Life?
Nay, cry aloud, and have no fear,
  We few against the world;
Awake, arise! the hope we bear
  Against the curse is hurled.

It grows and grows — are we the same,
  The feeble band, the few?
Or what are these with eyes aflame,
  And hands to deal and do?
This is the host that bears the word,
  "No master high or low" —
A lightning flame, a shearing sword,
  A storm to overthrow.

V. THE INDEPENDENT SELF

Self Determination

Alexis de Tocqueville: *Democracy In America*

AUTHOR AND TEXT: *Alexis de Tocqueville (1805-1859) was a French historian and politician, who spent a year (1831-32) in the United States to study the penal system of this young nation. From 1835 until 1840 he published the book which made him famous:* Democracy in America. *The following selection is taken from the second part of this work; the translation is by Henry Reeve (1813-1895).*

SELF-DETERMINATION AND CULTURAL HERITAGE: *De Tocqueville's observations raise the question of whether an accumulated cultural heritage, as deposited in libraries, museums, or schools, is a help or an impediment for the development of a person's self—a dead weight or the building material for a rich existence. There are those who argue that the acquisition of a learned education is likely to kill spontaneity, self-expression, and intellectual mobility, and there are those who argue that without any knowledge and understanding of past cultures people are empty, dull, narrow-minded, and intellectually even more immobile. And both parties to the argument have their repugnant scenarios which they try to avoid: the one a society where people hide their personal timidity, deadness, and lack of creativity behind a screen of acquired knowledge and tastes, the other a situation where human interaction is reduced to the happy spontaneity of higher apes who cannot perceive anything which goes beyond their most immediate impulses and needs. (At the beginning of the twentieth century, revolutionary socialists sometimes discussed among themselves the question of whether the coming revolution should abolish the entire culture of the society against which they were fighting, or only the rulers and oppressive institutions, while guarding the fine arts, e.g., as treasures of the past.)*

In dealing with this complex question the following considerations would be relevant: Familiarity with a cultural heritage does not necessarily mean that one's own spontaneity is stifled by it. As almost everything else (technology, e.g.), a cultural heritage can be used as well as misused. One can imitatively reproduce cultural activities, but one can also develop a number of creative responses to it. Also, a cultural heritage consists of many different kinds of things, some of which may be negligible, while others (such as language) may be crucial even for mere survival. Instead of talking about cultural heritage as a monolithic entity, it may be much more fruitful to talk about the usefulness or value of individual books, specific activities such as dancing, and so forth.

Finally, a very basic consideration is this: In order to live at all, we have to perceive things and think about them, and for this we need concepts. Even very low-level perceptions and communications presuppose a conceptual framework; no human being can exist with an entirely blank mind. These concepts are the heritage of some culture. From this fact conservative thinkers have concluded that one cannot liberate one's self from the past and one's cultural heritage in the way Enlightenment philosophers envisaged. Because to give up these things is tantamount to giving up thinking and perceiving altogether. But this conservative conclusion assumes that everything one inherits from one's own (or other people's) past is of the same kind. It assumes that by inheriting the language and certain basic concepts of a particular culture one thereby also inherits a commitment to certain values and institutions of that culture—which simply is not the case. It is quite possible to master a culture's language and concepts, and have at the same time a quite critical attitude toward its values, institutions, and history. The Enlightenment, after all, is part of Western Culture just as much as its absolute monarchs and the burning of "witches." One can say, in fact, that the rejection of one's own culture in a certain sense is part of that culture; the self-criticism of a civilization is one of its most civilized activities. It is for this reason that it may not be an exaggeration to say that the critics of a culture often did more for its preservation than its conservative defenders, namely by keeping it alive and moving. And an individual who "rejects culture" in the interest of self-development may be much closer to the heart of that culture than the archivists who consume themselves in preserving its external manifestations.

~ ~ ~

I think that in no country in the civilized world is less attention paid to philosophy than in the United States. The Americans have no philosophical school of their own; and they care but little for all the schools into which Europe is divided, the very names of which are scarcely known to them.

Nevertheless it is easy to perceive that almost all the inhabitants of the United States conduct their understanding in the same manner, and govern it by the same rules, that is to say, that without ever having taken the trouble to define the rules of a philosophical method, they are in possession of one, common to the whole people.

To evade the bondage of system and habit, of family-maxims, class-opinions, and in some degree, of national prejudices; to accept tradition only as a means of information, and existing facts only as a lesson used in doing otherwise and doing better; to seek the reason of things for oneself, and in oneself alone; to tend to results without being bound to means, and to aim at the substance through the form; — such are the principal characteristics of what I shall call the philosophical method of the Americans. But if I go further, and if I seek among those characteristics the principal one which includes almost all the rest, I discover that, in most operations of the mind, each American appeals only to the individual effort of his own understanding.

America is therefore one of the countries in the world where philosophy is least studied, and where the precepts of Descartes are best applied. Nor is this surprising. The Americans do not read the works of Descartes, because their social condition deters them from speculative studies; but they follow his maxims, because this very social condition naturally disposes their understanding to adopt them.

In the midst of the continual movement which agitates a democratic community, the tie which unites one generation to another is relaxed or broken; every man readily loses the trace of the ideas of his forefathers or takes no care about them.

Nor can men living in this state of society derive their belief from the opinions of the class to which they belong; for, so to speak, there are no longer any classes, or those which still exist are composed of such mobile elements, that their body can never exercise a real control over its members.

As to the influence which the intelligence of one man has on that of another, it must necessarily be very limited in a country where the citizens, placed on a footing of a general similitude, are all closely seen by each other; and where, as no signs of incontestable greatness or superiority are perceived in any one of them, they are constantly brought back to their own reason as the most obvious and proximate source of truth. It is not only confidence in this or that man which is then destroyed, but the taste for trusting the *ipse dixit* of any man whatsoever. Every one shuts himself up in his own breast, and affects from that point to judge the world.

The practice which obtains among the Americans of fixing the standard of their judgment in themselves alone, leads them to other habits of mind. As they perceive that they succeed in resolving without assistance all the little difficulties which their practical life presents, they readily conclude that everything in the world may be explained, and that nothing in it transcends the limits of the understanding. Thus they fall to denying what they cannot comprehend; which leaves them but little faith for whatever is supernatural. As it is on their own testimony that they are accustomed to rely, they like to discern the object which engages their attention with extreme clearness: they therefore strip off as much as possible all that covers it, they rid themselves of whatever separates them from it, they remove whatever conceals it from sight, in order to view it more closely and in the broad light of day. This disposition of the mind soon leads them to condemn forms, which they regard as useless and inconvenient veils placed between them and the truth. The Americans, then, have not required to extract their philosophical method from books; they have found it in themselves. The same thing may be remarked in what has taken place in Europe. This same method has only been established and made popular in Europe in proportion as the condition of society has become more equal, and men have grown more like each other. Let us consider for a moment the connection of the periods in which this change may be traced.

In the sixteenth century the Reformers subjected some of the dogmas of the ancient faith to the scrutiny of private judgment; but they still withheld from it the discussion of all the rest. In the seventeenth century, Bacon in the natural sciences, and Descartes in the study of philosophy in the strict sense of the term, abolished recognized formulas, destroyed the empire of tradition, and overthrew the authority of the schools. The philosophers of the eighteenth century, generalizing at length the same principle, undertook to submit to the private judgment of each man all the objects of his belief.

Who does not perceive that Luther, Descartes, and Voltaire employed the same method, and that they differed only in the greater or lesser use which they professed should be made of it? Why did the Reformers confine themselves so closely within the circle of religious ideas? Why did Descartes, choosing only to apply his method to certain matters, though he had made it fit to be applied to all, declare that men might judge for themselves in matters philosophical but not in matters political? How happened it that in the eighteenth century those general applications were all at once drawn from this same method, which Descartes and his predecessors had either not perceived or had rejected? To what, lastly, is the fact to be attributed, that at this period the method we are speaking of suddenly emerged from the schools, to penetrate into society and become the common standard of intelligence; and that, after it had become popular among the French, it has been ostensibly adopted or secretly followed by all the nations of Europe?

The philosophical method here designated may have been engendered in the sixteenth century—it may have been more accurately defined and more extensively applied in the seventeenth; but neither in the one nor in the other could it be commonly adopted. Political laws, the condition of society, and the habits of mind which are derived from these causes, were as yet opposed to it. It was discovered at a time when men were beginning to equalize and assimilate their conditions. It could only be generally followed in ages when those conditions had at length become nearly equal, and men nearly alike.

The philosophical method of the eighteenth century is then not only French, but it is democratic; and this explains why it was so readily admitted throughout Europe, where it has contributed so powerfully to change the face of society. It is not because the French have changed their former opinions, and altered their former manners, that they have convulsed the world; but because they were the first to generalize and bring to light a philosophical method, by the assistance of which it became easy to attack all that was old and to open a path to all that was new.

If it be asked why, at the present day, this same method is more rigorously followed and more frequently applied by the French than by the Americans, although the principle of equality be no less complete, and of more ancient date, among the latter people, the fact may be attributed to two circumstances, which it is essential to have clearly understood in the first instance.

It must never be forgotten that religion gave birth to Anglo-American society. In the United States religion is therefore mingled with all the habits of the nation and all the feelings of patriotism; whence it derives a peculiar force. To this powerful reason, another of no less intensity may be added: in America religion has, as it were, laid down its own limits. Religious institutions have remained wholly distinct from political institutions, so that former laws have been easily changed while former belief has remained unshaken. Christianity has therefore retained a strong hold on the public mind in America; and, I would more particularly remark, that its sway is not only that of a philosophical doctrine which has been adopted upon inquiry, but of a religion which is believed without discussion: In the United States, Christian sects are infinitely diversified and perpetually modified; but Christianity itself is a fact so irresistably established, that no one undertakes either to attack or to defend it. The Americans, having admitted the principal doctrines of the Christian religion without inquiry, are obliged to accept in like manner a great number of moral truths originating in it and connected with it. Hence the activity of individual analysis is restrained within narrow limits, and many of the most important of human opinions are removed from the range of its influence.

The second circumstance to which I have alluded is the following: the social condition and the constitution of the Americans are democratic, but they have not had a democratic revolution. They arrived upon the soil they occupy in nearly the condition in which we see them at the present day; and this is of very considerable importance.

There are no revolutions which do not shake existing belief, enervate authority, and throw doubts over commonly received ideas. The effect of all revolutions is therefore, more or less, to surrender men to their own guidance, and to open to the mind of every man a void and almost unlimited range of speculation. When equality of conditions succeeds a protracted conflict between the different classes of which the elder society was composed, envy, hatred and uncharitableness, pride and exaggerated self-confidence are apt to seize upon the human heart, and plant their sway there for a time. This, independently of equality itself, tends powerfully to divide men — to lead them to mistrust the judgment of others, and to seek the light of truth nowhere but in their own understandings. Every one then attempts to be his own sufficient guide, and makes it his boast to form his own opinions on all subjects. Men are no longer bound together by ideas, but by interests; and it would seem as if human opinions were reduced to a sort of intellectual dust, scattered on every side, unable to collect, unable to cohere.

Thus, that independence of mind which equality supposes to exist, is never so great, nor ever appears so excessive, as at the time when equality is beginning to establish itself, and in the course of that painful labour by which it is established. That sort of intellectual freedom which equality may give, ought therefore to be very carefully distinguished from the anarchy which revolution brings.

Each of these two things must be severally considered, in order not to conceive exaggerated hopes or fears of the future.

I believe that men who will live under the new forms of society will make frequent use of their private judgment; but I am far from thinking that they will often abuse it. This is attributable to a cause of more general application to all democratic countries, and which, in the long run, must needs restrain in them the independence of individual speculation within fixed, and sometimes narrow, limits.

Johann W. Goethe: "To The United States"

In comparison to his "Prometheus," this poem (written in 1818) is very light. (The original has rhymes, and sounds, therefore, much more playful.) But it expresses well the European image of America as an unencumbered, new world:

America, you are better off
Than our continent, the old one;
You have no crumbling castles,
Nor rocks of basalt;
You are not hampered
At lively times
By useless memories
And vain disputes.

Use the present well!
And should your children once write verse,
May they be shielded by a gentle fate
From stories of knights, robbers and ghosts.

James M. Whitfield: "America"

The European view of America was, of course, rather one-sided. It did not take very much into consideration the fate of the American Indians, and it neglected the blatant hypocrisy which the white settlers displayed toward their imported black slaves. As the supposed equality of all human beings as rational beings was disregarded in Europe with respect to women, it was disregarded in the United States with regard to black people as well. The black poet, James M. Whitfield, exposes the discrepancy between Enlightenment pretense and the depressing reality of slavery in his famous poem "America."

Whitfield (1830-1870) was born in New York City, but apparently spent most of his life in Buffalo, New York. He made a living as a barber, until he gained some fame with his book America and Other Poems. He became an advocate of black emigration to Central America as a solution to America's race problem. He died in obscurity.

America, it is to thee,
Thou boasted land of liberty, —
It is to thee I raise my song,
Thou land of blood, and crime, and wrong.
It is to thee my native land,
From which has issued many a band
To tear the black man from his soil,
And force him here to delve and toil;
Chained on your blood-bemoistened sod,
Cringing beneath a tyrant's rod,
Stripped of those rights which Nature's God
  Bequeathed to all the human race,
Bound to a petty tyrant's nod,
  Because he wears a paler face.
Was it for this that freedom's fires
Were kindled by your patriot sires?

Was it for this they shed their blood,
On hill and plain, on field and flood?
Was it for this that wealth and life
Were staked upon that desperate strife,
Which drenched this land for seven long years
With blood of men, and women's tears?
When black and white fought side by side,
  Upon the well contested field, —
Turned back the fierce opposing tide,
  And made the proud invader yield —
When, wounded, side by side they lay,
  And heard with joy the proud hurrah
From their victorious comrades say
  That they had waged successful war,
The thought ne'er entered in their brains
That they endured those toils and pains,
To forge fresh fetters, heavier chains
For their own children, in whose veins
Should flow that patriotic blood,
So freely shed on field and flood.
Oh, no; they fought, as they believed,
  For the inherent rights of man;
But mark, how they have been deceived
  By slavery's accursed plan.
They never thought, when thus they shed
  Their heart's best blood, in freedom's cause,
That their own sons would live in dread,
  Under unjust, oppressive laws:
That those who quietly enjoyed
  The rights for which they fought and fell,
Could be the framers of a code,
  That would disgrace the fiends of hell!
Could they have looked, with prophet's ken,
  Down to the present evil time,
  Seen free-born men, uncharged with crime,
Consigned unto a slaver's pen, —
Or thrust into a prison cell,
With thieves and murderers to dwell —
While that same flag whose stripes and stars
Had been their guide through freedom's wars
As proudly waved above the pen

Of dealers in the souls of men!
Or could the shades of all the dead,
  Who fell beneath that starry flag,
Visit the scenes where they once bled,
  On hill and plain, on vale and crag,
By peaceful brook, or ocean's strand,
  By inland lake, or dark green wood,
Where'er the soil of this wide land
  Was moistened by their patriot blood,—
And then survey the country o'er,
  From north to south, from east to west,
And hear the agonizing cry
Ascending up to God on high,
From western wilds to ocean's shore,
  The fervent prayer of the oppressed.
And manhood, too, with soul of fire,
And arm of strength, and smothered ire,
Stands pondering with brow of gloom,
Upon his dark unhappy doom,
Whether to plunge in battle's strike,
And buy his freedom with his life,
And with stout heart and weapon strong,
Pay back the tyrant wrong for wrong
Or wait the promised time of God,
  When his Almighty ire shall wake,
And smite the oppressor in his wrath,
And hurl red ruin in his path,
And with the terrors of his rod,
  Cause adamantine hearts to quake.
Here Christian writhes in bondage still,
  Beneath his brother Christian's rod,
And pastors trample down at will,
  The image of the living God.

*

Almighty God! thy aid impart,
And fire anew each faltering heart,
And strengthen every patriot's hand,
Who aims to save our native land.
We do not come before thy throne,

With carnal weapons drenched in gore,
Although our blood has freely flown,
  In adding to the tyrant's store.
Father! before thy throne we come,
  Not in panoply of war,
With pealing trump, and rolling drum,
  And cannon booming loud and far;
Striving in blood to wash out blood,
  Through wrong to seek redress for wrong;
For while thou'rt holy, just and good,
  The battle is not to the strong;
But in the sacred name of peace,
  Of justice, virtue, love and truth,
We pray, and never mean to cease,
  Till weak old age and fiery youth
In freedom's cause their voices raise,
And burst the bonds of every slave;
Till, north and south, and east and west,
The wrongs we bear shall be redressed.

Ralph W. Emerson: "Give All To Love"

In this amazingly modern poem of 1847, Emerson advocates an apparently paradoxical position: On the one hand he recommends following the passions of one's love unconditionally, to give up everything else in one's life for one's love. On the other hand he recommends resisting the temptation to make the beloved person one's own, to turn her or him into a quasi-eternal possession. On the one hand one's life is to consist of loving her or him, on the other hand one is to respect totally the beloved person's separateness and independence. On the one hand the beloved person is to be all, on the other, one is ultimately to be centered in one's self. There seems to be a contradiction in these recommendations.

If Emerson were a rationalist, the two demands would not necessarily contradict each other. In Kant's thinking, e.g., the drive to possess another person would simply be construed as part of one's irrational emotions, while the rule to respect another person's independence would be a demand of reason. And a mature person would, of course, in the end follow the demand of reason, repressing any irrational urges as much as possible. In this way the Enlightenment culture generally played down the importance of passion and emotions, allowing the latter at most as a kind of foolishness of the young, or as temporary outbursts in adults. (This is how Mary Wollstonecraft, e.g., represents the passions of love.) But Emerson was not a rationalist; in his view a person's real self is identical with one's deepest instincts and emotions. Since the passions of love belong to the most deeply seated human feelings, Emerson recommends going with these passions as far as possible, to disregard "friends, kindred, days, estate," etc. in favor of one's love. This, however, seems to contradict his advice to not to try to hold on to the beloved person by every possible means. If the feelings of love are valid, then the desire to possess seems to be valid also.

The solution to this puzzle has to do with Emerson's conception of self as activity, as kinetic energy, as it were. A person is himself or herself when actually feeling, seeing, thinking, doing, and so forth. A person ceases to be himself or herself when one invests one's self in something external, such as properties, institutions, or rank. In doing so the state of being active is likely to come to an end, and the person loses as a person. Wealth may impress many people, but it more often than not hides the poverty of the owner. High rank may command considerable respect in the world, but often enough it disguises a person who has become lazy and unimaginative. The only thing which ought to count, according to Emerson, is the state and the nature of the person himself or herself.

Thus, what counts in someone's love is the actual loving, and the intensive communication between the lovers. As soon as the beloved person becomes something like a secure possession, the actual feelings are likely to become weak, and the communication routine. The external props of a relationship replace the inner life; Being is replaced by Having — to use Erich Fromm's language. The atrophy of the life forces may set in, and the dominance of dead and ossified structures will be the result.

A love relationship should last as long as the mutual feelings are intensive and alive; beyond these feelings there simply is no real relationship. This conviction is one reason for the particular recommendations of Emerson's in this poem. Another reason is his conviction that all feelings ought to be felt as purely as possible, the agreeable ones as well as the painful ones. Every part of one's life has to be perceived with full alertness; nothing ought to be hidden or covered up. In the words of his friend Thoreau: "Be it life or death, we crave only reality. If we are really dying, let us hear the rattle in our throats and feel cold in the extremities; if we are alive, let us go about our business" (Walden, Chapter II). Only with this openness to one's actual situation will reality reveal itself, will the ultimate insights come. Even if the center of one's feelings, the beloved person, is lost, something even more awesome will open up: "When half-gods go, the gods arrive."

Give all to love;
Obey thy heart;
Friends, kindred, days,
Estate, good-fame,
Plans, credit and the Muse—
Nothing refuse.

'T is a brave master;
Let it have scope:
Follow it utterly,
Hope beyond hope:
High and more high
It dives into noon,
With wing unspent,
Untold intent;
But it is a god,
Knows its own path
And the outlets of the sky.

It was never for the mean;
It requireth courage stout.
Souls above doubt,
Valor unbending,
It will reward—
They shall return
More than they were,
And ever ascending.

Leave all for love;
Yet, hear me, yet,
One word more thy heart behoved,
One pulse more of firm endeavor—
Keep thee to-day,
To-morrow, forever,
Free as an Arab
Of thy beloved.

Cling with life to the maid;
But when the surprise,
First vague shadow of surmise
Flits across her bosom young,
Of a joy apart from thee,
Free be she, fancy-free;
Nor thou detain her vesture's hem,
Nor the palest rose she flung
From her summer diadem.

Though thou loved her as thyself,
As a self of purer clay,
Though her parting dims the day,
Stealing grace from all alive;
Heartily know,
When half-gods go,
The gods arrive.

VI. THE SELF AS AGENT OF HISTORY

Self Determination

Georg W. F. Hegel: *The Phenomenology Of The Spirit*

AUTHOR AND TEXT: *Georg Wilhelm Friedrich Hegel (1770-1831) was one of the most typical thinkers of the nineteenth century, mainly on account of his emphasis on historical development in the explanation of natural and cultural history. He began his studies in the theological seminary at the University of Tubingen (where the poet Friedrich Hölderlin was one of his classmates), made a living as editor and private tutor, taught a year at the University of Jena (from where Fichte had been fired a few years earlier), and finally became full professor at the University of Berlin, where he was what his critics call "the Prussian State Philosopher." He was the author of a monumental, all-embracing philosophical system, and of a method which tries to explain everything in nature and history in terms of a dialectical process, i.e., a process in which everything undergoes the stages of being thesis, antithesis and synthesis, before turning into a thesis again. (Thus, personal histories, as well as histories of whole peoples, can be philosophically construed as going through a stage of complete domination by a father figure or absolute ruler (=thesis), then through a stage of total rebellion in which all authorities and inherited values are rejected (=antithesis), and finally through a stage of a wise combination of both (=synthesis) — before going through another developmental cycle on a higher level.) It was this dialectical method (later adopted by Marx) which made Hegel most famous, and which fits him so well into the nineteenth century with its pronounced historical, evolutionary thinking.*

The major part of the text below is taken from Hegel's first large work, The Phenomenology of the Spirit *(the chapter on "Virtue and the Ways of the World"), which he finished on the day in 1806 when Napoleon defeated the Prussian army near Jena. The book is a philosophical reconstruction of the evolution of human consciousness from mere sense perception through morality, art and religion to absolute knowledge. The passages excerpted below deal with the moral and political ideals of the revolutionaries of his time.*

THE SELF AS AGENT OF HISTORY

Hegel's language, particularly in his first book, is forbiddingly technical and opaque. The Phenomenology *is one of those books where philosophers traditionally spend a whole semester on deciphering and explaining a few pages. Since there is no room in the present context to explain Hegel's complicated conceptual apparatus, the following translation is relatively liberal and interpretive. The first section of the text is from the* Phenomenology, *the two added sections are from Hegel's introduction to his* Outline of the Philosophy of Law *(1821).*

IDEAL AND REALITY: *Traditionally the two are considered as separate entities with different forms of existence, which usually stand in opposition to each other. In Plato's philosophy, to which Hegel alludes here in part, the ideal had a "higher" degree of reality than ordinary objects, the latter being nothing but the " shadows" of their original ideas. An idealist in this sense is a person who lives in such a way as if ideals were closer to and more relevant for the human self than the world of the senses. Hegel saw the reformers and revolutionaries of his day as such idealists who considered the idea of freedom as more real than the existing states and social relations; he attacked them as unworldly dreamers who would be better off if they studied and respected the institutions which history had created. And such slogans as "Liberty, Equality, Fraternity" he discounted as mere rhetoric and, if analyzed, literally meaningless phrases.*

Hegel, however, is himself an Idealist; he sees himself as the inheritor of the preparatory work of Kant and Fichte. But his Idealism comes in the disguise of a seemingly materialistic interpretation of history. While Kant and other Idealists were concerned with the deduction of principles from pure reason, and with their possible realization in a world hostile to ideas, Hegel proposes to forget such ideas and to investigate the real movements of power in history instead. Only by comprehending what happens in the real world will one gain any worthwhile insights. But by grasping the real conditions and their historical genesis (and here Hegel's idealism comes to the surface) one will find that they are the work of what he called the "World Spirit," that this spirit expresses itself in material, historical form. "World history is the expression of the divine and absolute process of the spirit in its highest form, of the progression whereby it discovers its true nature and becomes conscious of itself," as he stated it in one of his lectures in 1822. Thus, as a true Hegelian Idealist, one must refrain from willfully projecting one's own ideas onto history (as the revolutionaries did), and limit one's self to the faithful study of the sequence of historical events without preconceptions. (Not in the way of assembling disconnected facts, however, but by seeing them in their comprehensive, evolutionary order.) Reason is to be found in the way things actually are, not in the way things ought to be according to people's minds. *"What is reasonable, that is real; and what is real, that is reasonable,"* Hegel wrote in the introduction to the Outline of the Philosophy of Law. Thus, in his philosophy there is no real distinction between ideal and reality.

It was this understanding of matters which put Hegel into the camp of the conservatives. For what he was conveying to the reading public was the assurance that the Prussian monarchy was basically all right the way it was, and that its critics (mostly students and professors, but also numerous laborers, peasants, and newspaper editors, all of whom were censored, spied upon, persecuted, imprisoned, or driven into exile) were immature dreamers who did not understand the world. True wisdom, according to his thinking, will not try to change the world, but rather understand it.

THE SELF AND HISTORY: *Obviously, within this conceptual framework self-realization is not to be achieved in the way Kant or Fichte thought about it, namely by emancipating one's self from limiting, external determinations. On the contrary, for Hegel self-realization can only be gained by aligning one's self thoroughly with the specific historical and social conditions into which one has been born. For him there is no such thing as standing mentally above a situation, and criticizing it from the outside. One is a citizen of Prussia, a member of a particular family, a member of a social class, and a European at a certain point in history, and all attempts to deny or downgrade these facts of one's life are in vain. The only difference between an individual's fixed position in the medieval world and that of a modern self is the possibility that the latter can assume his or her position consciously and* willingly, while people in the Middle Ages lived under their conditions naively and without the modern knowledge of history. The modern self knows his or her place to be limited and partial, but also understands that the universal World Spirit achieves its goal through the activities of such partial individuals and forces. The attempt of Enlightenment philosophers to limit the partiality of individuals by obliging them to act according to general, rational principles is both unnecessary and futile. People are the agents of the universal World Spirit without their own attempt to become such universally-minded beings.

This is why Hegel affirms so strongly individualism and egoism — in a way reminiscent of the ideas of Adam Smith's The Wealth of Nations *(1776). Smith maintains that if everyone in a capitalistic economy will vigorously pursue his or her own interest without regard for the welfare of others, then the net effect for the whole system will be such that everyone will be better off. Regulative interference in this system of individual egoism, even if well-intentioned, will only hamper the economic progress from which, in the end, everyone will benefit. Similarly Hegel asserts that the higher reason of history will create an ever more reasonable world, even if all the acting individuals should have no idea of what they are ultimately involved in. They may think that they are merely pursuing their own personal advantage, but in reality they are acting as the agents of the World Spirit: by doing the one, they are also doing the other. Self-realization, then, does not consist in determining one's fate independently of the circumstances in which one may find oneself, but in making one's self the conscious agent of history by acting out the role provided by these circumstances.*

~ ~ ~

Virtue, then, will be vanquished by the ways of the world, because its goal is an abstract, unreal essence, and because its endeavors are based on distinctions which exist only in words. It intended to exist by sacrificing individuality, but reality cannot be found anywhere except in individuals. The Good was to be that which is real, and which is opposed to the actual state of the world. But the actual state of the world is what is truly real. What is supposedly real is conceived as an abstraction which is pitted against the actual state of affairs. But an abstraction is just an abstraction, and it does not really exist—except as an entity in the mind. That which truly exists is that which is commonly called real, for what is real is essentially that which exists for others, i.e., being. But the consciousness of virtue is founded on the distinction between that which really exists in itself, and being—a distinction without truth.

The ways of the world supposedly are the perversion of the Good, because individualism is their basic principle. But individualism is the principle of reality, for through it everything essential becomes accessible to others. The ways of the world may pervert the Unchangeable (the Good), but by doing so they convert it from the nothingness of abstraction to the being of reality.

The ways of the world, then, are victorious over that which virtue pits against them; they vanquish something which assumes a mere abstraction to be something essential. They are victorious not over something real, but over fabricated distinctions which do not exist, over those pompous speeches concerning the Best of Humanity, the latter's suppression, sacrifices for the Good, and the misuse of human potentials. Such ideal essences and purposes collapse as so many empty words which elevate the heart, but leave the mind empty, which edify without being constructive—declamations which have only one content: the conviction that the person who pretends to act for such noble purposes, and who utters such magificent words, is himself a magificent character (an aggrandizement which enlarges his and other people's heads—with a lot of hot air).

In antiquity virtue had a definite and secure meaning, for it was materially grounded in the substance of a people, and it had as its purpose a real and already existing good. For this reason it was also not directed against all of reality as a perversion, against the ways of the world. But the virtue we are talking about here has lost touch with any such substance, has therefore no essence; it is a virtue of imagination and empty words. This empty rhetoric which does battle with the ways of the world would be exposed immediately if one pressed for the clarification of its slogans; in consequence these slogans are presumed to be self-evident. The demand to state explicitly what is evident will be answered with a deluge of new slogans, or with a reference to the heart which supposedly reveals inwardly what the slogans mean. Which simply amounts to admitting one's inability to say what they mean. — In an unconscious way the insignificance of this rhetoric has already come to be taken for granted in the culture of these days. For the interest in these slogans, and in the habit of aggrandizing one's self with them, has vanished completely — a loss which manifests itself by their provoking nothing but a yawn.

The result of the above battle, then, is that consciousness leaves the notion of a Good, which has yet to gain reality, behind like an empty coat. In its struggle it has learned that the ways of the world are not so bad, after all, for their reality is the reality of the Universal (World Spirit). Through this learning experience the means for achieving the Good by sacrificing individuality vanishes, for individuality is exactly the realization of the ideal. And the state of the actual world ceases to be considered as a perversion of the Good, for it is nothing else than the conversion of a mere goal into reality. The actions of individuals are the reality of the Universal.

With this, however, the ways of the world, which were opposed to the thought of the ideal, are vanquished as well. The self-centeredness of individualism was opposed to what is essential, to the Universal, and thus appeared to be a reality separated from what is truly real. But after it has become clear that the actual world is inseparably united with the Universal, the separateness of the ways of the world, and the absoluteness of virtue, are both only partial aspects of the matter. The individualism of the everyday world may harbor the opinion that everyone acts only for himself, egoistically, but it is actually better than it thinks it is, for its actions are at the same time deeds of a universally valid kind. When individualism behaves egoistically, the individuals simply do not know what they do. And when the latter pronounce that all the people act egoistically, then they only say that people have no consciousness of what their activity really is.

*

Thus, this treatise, in as much as it deals with the Theory of the State, is nothing but the attempt to comprehend and describe the State as something which is in itself reasonable. As a philosophical treatise, it definitely has to stay away from trying to construe the State as it ought to be. If it is to teach anything, it is not to tell the State how it ought to be, but how it can be understood as a moral universe.

Hic Rhodus, hic saltus.
(Here is Rhodes, here dance!)

To comprehend that which actually exists — that is the task of philosophy. For what exists, that is reason.

*

To say just one more word about the teaching of how the world ought to be: philosophy will always be too late for that in any event. As the thought of the world, it will always appear in the time after reality has already completed its process of creation. This insight, which is found by reflection, is also taught by history. The ideal will appear as the counterpart of reality only when the latter has matured; only then will philosophy understand the world, and, grasping its substance, construe it as an intellectual empire. When philosophy paints its grey-in-grey, then a figure of life has already grown old, and with its grey colors it cannot be made young again, but only comprehended. The owl of Minerva will not begin its flight until nightfall.

Philip Freneau: "On Mr. Paine's *Rights Of Man*"

Freneau (1752-1832) is sometimes called "the father of American Poetry." He made a living as journalist, farmer, sea captain, and tinker. During the American Revolution he gained fame for his vitriolic poems against the British. After the Revolution he aligned himself with the Jeffersonian Democrats, while the country was ruled by the conservative Federalists under Hamilton, who wanted to limit popular rule as much as possible. Freneau, because of his reputation as an outspoken Liberal, fell on hard times. Most of his prose and poetry was published by himself on his own hand press. He died in poverty and obscurity.

Paine's Rights of Man *ran serially in a New York paper in 1791. By that time Paine himself suffered much from his liberal reputation in a country which had turned noticeably conservative. Freneau's poem appeared at the end of the last installment of Paine's text. Freneau hoped that the publication of* Rights of Man *would stem the conservative tide in the United States.*

The poem represents the kind of liberalism and idealism against which Hegel's conservative remarks are directed. It expresses the Enlightenment enthusiasm, that, toward the end of the eighteenth century, had begun to be "vanquished by the ways of the world," in Europe as well as in the United States.

> Thus briefly sketched the sacred RIGHTS OF MAN,
> How inconsistent with the ROYAL PLAN!
> Which for itself exclusive honour craves,
> Where some are master born, and millions slaves.
> With what contempt must every eye look down
> On that base, childish bauble called a crown,
> The gilded bait, that lures the crowd, to come,
> Bow down their necks, and meet a slavish doom;
> The source of half the miseries men endure,
> The quack that kills them, while it seems to cure.

Self Determination

Roused by the REASON of his manly page,
Once more shall PAINE a listening world engage:
From Reason's source, a bold reform he brings,
In raising up mankind, he pulls down kings,
Who, source of discord, patrons of all wrong.
On blood and murder have been fed too long:
Hid from the world, and tutored to be base,
The curse, the scourge, the ruin of our race,
Their's was the task, a dull designing few,
To shackle beings that they scarcely knew,
Who made this globe the residence of slaves,
And built their thrones on systems formed by knaves
— Advance, bright years, to work their final fall,
And haste the period that shall crush them all.
 Who, that has read and scann'd the historic page
But glows, at every line, with kindling rage.
To see by them the rights of men aspersed,
Freedom restrain'd, and Nature's law reversed,
Men, ranked with beasts, by monarchs will'd away,
And bound young fools, or madmen to obey:
Now driven to wars, and now oppressed at home,
Compelled in crowds o'er distant seas to roam,
From India's climes the plundered prize to bring
To glad the strumpet, or to glut the king.
 COLUMBIA, hail! immmortal be thy reign:
Without a king, we till the smiling plain;
Without a king, we trace the unbounded sea,
And traffic round the globe, through each degree;
Each foreign clime our honour'd flag reveres,
Which asks no monarch, to support the STARS:
Without a king, the laws maintain their sway,
While honour bids each generous heart obey.
Be ours the task the ambitious to restrain,
And this great lesson teach — that kings are vain;
That warring realms to certain ruin haste,
That kings subsist by war, and wars are waste:
So shall our nation, form'd on Virtue's plan,
Remain the guardian of the Rights of Man,
A vast Republic, famed through every clime,
Without a king, to see the end of time.

George Gordon, Lord Byron:
"When A Man Hath No Freedom To Fight For At Home"

George Gordon (1788-1824) was a writer and freedom-fighter whose short life was filled with adventures, fame, notoriety, and deeply felt relationships. At the age of twenty one he became a member of the House of Lords, made an adventurous journey across the Mediterranean world, became famous with his "Childe Harold" (1812), in which he described his travels, was the darling of London society, and then (because of the scandalous course of his marriage) its scapegoat. In 1816 he left England—forever, as it turned out. For several years he was in close contact with the circle around Shelley and Wollstonecraft, with whom he founded and edited the Liberal. *In 1823 he left for Greece, where he financed and led a group of fighters that participated in the uprising against the Turkish occupation. He died in Greece after a period of illness, probably from meningitis.*

Lord Byron was deeply committed to the cause of liberty everywhere. At the same time he had a considerable ironic distance toward feelings of pathos and naive seriousness—including his own commitments. He often combines in his attitude deep passion with the critical and sarcastic exposure of this passion. The following poem exemplifies this ambiguity:

When a man hath no freedom to fight for at home,
Let him combat for that of his neighbors;
Let him think of the glories of Greece and Rome,
And get knocked on the head for his labours.
To do good to Mankind is the chivalrous plan,
And is always as nobly requited;
Then battle for Freedom where ever you can,
And, if not shot or hanged, you'll get knighted.

4. Marx as Prometheus

VII. THE SELF AS THE MAKER OF THE HUMAN WORLD

SELF DETERMINATION

Karl Marx: "Alienated Labor"

AUTHOR AND TEXT: *Karl Marx (1818-1883) grew up in Germany under the same conservative conditions under which Kant, Fichte and Hegel had lived, and as a student at the University of Berlin he joined a political club that advocated political democracy. Very soon after his graduation he became familiar, however, with ideas which went beyond mere political reforms, namely types of socialism or communism,* i.e., *economic reforms. For the rest of his life he dedicated himself to the radical restructuring of modern society, living most of the time in exile, in London. Marx found that most socialist revolutionaries had moral objections to capitalism, and all kinds of utopian ideas of how to overcome it, but no understanding of how a capitalist economy actually works. He also found that he did not understand capitalism himself. For this reason he spent two decades studying and researching in the library of the British Museum, after which he published his most famous work,* Capital, *in 1864. (As he was personally much more interested in philosophy, literature, and mathematics, than in economics, he hated most of the time spent on this work.)*

It was only in the twentieth century that scholars found an unpublished study by Marx, the so-called Economic and Philosophical Manuscripts of 1844. *This study consists of somewhat disorganized, but very insightful notes which Marx jotted down while reading such classical economists as Adam Smith and David Ricardo. The study has since gained prominence because in it Marx formulated explicitly his theory of alienation,* i.e., *his analysis of how people become inevitably estranged from their own selves under the conditions of capitalist production. The following selection is from the section "Alienated Labor" of the* Manuscripts of 1844.

WHAT KIND OF POVERTY DO WORKERS PRIMARILY SUFFER?: *Some of Marx' statements in his notes of 1844 seem very intriguing, if not patently false. "The worker becomes the poorer, the more wealth he produces," e.g., seems to fly in the face of the facts. During the Industrial Revolution, to be sure, workers lived under appalling conditions; fourteen hours of work per day, child labor, high accident rates, etc., were the norm. But these conditions could be, and have been, improved by reforms within capitalism, and today most workers in industrialized capitalist societies seem to enjoy a higher standard of living than even the rich of past ages. How can Marx say, then, that workers in all capitalist societies become the poorer the more they produce?*

To understand what Marx is aiming at one has to understand that Marx' highest value is not material consumption, but self-determination and self-realization. In Marx' philosophy standards of living are not defined in terms of more food, more drinks, more clothes, more vehicles, more appliances — in short: more things. A high standard of living rather means rich experiences, fully developed emotions, closeness, honesty, and intensity of human relations, wealth of insights, and so forth. A person with few possessions, but with the freedom to develop himself or herself, certainly comes closer to Marx' ideal than a well-paid worker who can afford to buy many consumer goods, but who is neither educated enough to understand the society in which he lives, nor has the will to shape, together with his colleagues, his working conditions or the political system under which he lives. Marx was not so much interested in what people have, but in what they are. He was interested in people being alive, informed and in control of their own destiny, instead of their being the manipulable material of powerful and anonymous organizations.

The worker's poverty, then, consists foremost of his or her lack of self-determination, as far as Marx is concerned. And this lack of self-determination increases the more "the worker" (i.e. the entire work force) produces. For through the accumulated labor of the work force the natural world is replaced by a man-made world, an artificial environment. But since workers do not own what they produce, this artificial environment is out of their control, confronting them as something alien. Human beings become increasingly dependent on something which human labor has created. And the more people produce the more they replace nature with an artificial environment, the more dependent they become.

In the twentieth century the nature of this lack of self-determination has become more obvious than ever. Millions of people, busy and thoughtless like ants, produce floods of merchandise, huge industries with their corresponding vast administrations, and awesome amounts of bombs, tanks, poisonous gas, etc. And periodically people are victimized by their own products without understanding how and why. They are haunted by economic crises, wedged-in and choked by ever expanding industries, and decimated by sophisticated war machines. At a time when human control over nature has progressed further than ever, most people are powerless, ignorant, discouraged, and apathetic. And that is the major kind of poverty from which they are suffering.

THE LOSS OF SELF BY LOSING ONE'S ACTIVITY: *Marx takes it for granted that one's activity is an essential part of one's self-realization. People would neither be themselves, nor happy, if they could not be active. But one's activity has to be under one's control to be part of self-realization. An artist, e.g., does not mind working hard and for many hours, because his or her work is meaningful in terms of self-expression and self-realization. Factory or office workers, by contrast, leave their work as soon as they can afford to, because it has little to do with their selves, because it is a mere means to make a living. Yet, most people use the better part of their lives to do work which has little to do with themselves as persons. They are tied to their work with their whole existence. But since their work is not theirs, they are alienated from themselves, i.e., they are not themselves for the greater part of their lives.*

Students, incidentally, have become like factory workers. For the most part they do not study to grow as persons, but to be rewarded for their toils with diplomas, status, and money. Studying has lost its intrinsic value, it has become a means to get something else. Self-alienation is even more pronounced here, because the innermost faculties of a student are harnessed in the pursuit of an external goal.

~ ~ ~

We have started with the premises of political economy. We have accepted its terminology and its laws.

We assumed the existence of private property, the separation of labor, capital, and land, also of wages, profit, and rent—likewise the division of labor, competition, the concept of exchange value, etc. Using political economy itself, its own concepts, we have shown that the worker sinks to the level of a commodity, and of the most wretched commodity at that, and that the misery of the worker is in inverse proportion to the power and greatness of his production, that the inevitable result of competition is the accumulation of capital in the hands of a few, and thus the terrifying restoration of monopoly, and that finally the difference between entrepreneur and landlord, like that between the agricultural worker and the factory worker, disappears, and that the whole of society is bound to fall apart into the two classes of owners and workers.

*

The worker becomes the poorer the more wealth he produces, the more his production increases in power and volume. The more commodities he creates, the cheaper a commodity he becomes. In direct proportion to the increase of value of the world of things progresses the devaluation of the human world. Labor produces not only commodities, it also produces itself, and the worker as a commodity—and this at the same rate as it produces commodities.

All this expresses only that the object which labor produces, its product, confronts it as something alien, as a power which exists independently of the producer. The product of labor is labor which transforms itself into an object, which becomes a thing, which is its objectification. The realization of labor appears as a loss of reality for the worker, objectification as a loss of object and dependence on it, appropriation as estrangement, as alienation.

The realization of labor appears so much as a loss of reality that workers lose it to the point of starving to death. Objectification appears so much as the loss of object that workers lose the necessary things not only for living, but also for working. In fact, work itself turns into an object which workers can obtain only with the most strenuous efforts, and with the most irregular interruptions. The appropriation of the object appears so much as alienation that workers can own the less the more they produce, and that to the same degree to which they are controlled by what they produce, *i.e.*, by capital.

All this results from the fact that the worker relates to the product of his labor as an alien object. For it is clear, on this premise, that the alien, objective world will become the more powerful the more the worker produces; and the poorer he becomes himself, his inner work, and the less he owns. It is the same in religion. The more humans put into God, the less they retain in themselves. The worker puts his life into his product; now it belongs no longer to him, but to the object. Thus the greater his activity, the greater is his lack of objects. Whatever the product of his labor is, he is not. Hence, the greater his product, the less he is himself. The alienation of the worker through his product does not only mean that his labor becomes an object, an external entity, but also that it exists outside of him, independently, as something alien, that it turns into a power on its own confronting him, that the life which he has given to his product stands against him as something strange and hostile.

Let us now take a closer look at the objectification, the production of the worker and its alienation, the loss of the object, of his product.

The worker cannot create anything without nature, without the sensuous external world. It is the material in which his labor realizes itself, in which it is active, from which and through which it produces.

Just as nature provides labor with the means of life in the sense that labor cannot live without objects on which to perform, it also provides the means of life in the narrower sense, *i.e.*, the means for the physical subsistence of the worker.

Hence, the more the worker by his labor appropriates the external world, sensuous nature, the more he deprives himself of means of life in a two-fold manner. First, the sensuous external world ceases more and more to be an object belonging to his labor, to be a means of life for his activity. Second, it ceases more and more to be a means of life in the immediate sense, a means for the physical subsistence of the laborer.

In this two-fold sense, then, the worker becomes dependent on the object of his labor: he receives an object of labor, *i.e.*, work, and he receives means of subsistence. He needs to exist as a worker, and he needs to exist as a physical creature. It is the height of his dependence that he can remain a physical creature only as a worker and that he can be a worker only as a physical entity.

(The alienation of the worker in his product is expressed in terms of political economy in the following way: the more the worker produces, the less he has to consume; the more values the worker creates, the less value and dignity he has himself; the better formed the worker's product becomes, the more deformed he becomes as a human being; the more civilized the product is, the more barbarous is its producer; the more powerful labor, the more impotent the laborer; the more sophisticated the work, the more stupid and dependent the worker.)

Political economy hides the alienation in the present shape of labor by ignoring the immediate relation between the worker (labor) and production. Labor, to be sure, produces marvelous things for the rich, but for the laborer it produces privation. It produces palaces, but hovels for the worker. It produces beauty, but cripples the worker. It replaces work by machines, but it throws part of the workforce back to a barbarous kind of work, while turning the others into machines. It produces sophistication, but for the workforce it produces feeble-mindedness and idiocy.

The immediate relation of labor to its product is the relation of workers to the products of their labor. The relation of the owners to the objects of production and to production itself is only a consequence of the first relationship; it confirms it. We will look at this latter aspect later. When we ask, then, what the essential relation of labor is, we are asking for the relation of the worker to production.

So far we have considered the estrangement, the alienation of the worker only in one respect, namely only with respect to his relation to the product of his labor. But alienation shows itself not only in the result, but also in the process of production, within the productive activity itself. How would the worker encounter the product of his activity as something alien, if he did not alienate himself from himself in the act of production? The product is, after all, only the summary of the activity, of production. If, then, the product of labor is alienation, then production itself is active alienation, the alienating of activity, the activity of alienation. In the alienation of the object of labor we only see the summary of estrangement, the alienation in the activity of work itself.

In what, then consists the alienation of labor?

First, in the fact that labor is external to the worker, *i.e.*, that it does not belong to his nature, that therefore he does not realize himself in his work, that he denies himself in it, that he does not feel at ease in it, but rather unhappy, that he does not develop any free physical or mental energy, but rather mortifies his flesh and ruins his spirit. The worker, therefore, is only himself when he does not work, and in his work he feels outside himself. He is at home when he is not working, and when he is working he is not at home. His labor, therefore, is not voluntary, but forced; forced labor. It is, therefore, not the gratification of a need, but only a means to gratify needs outside itself. It's alien nature shows itself clearly by the fact that work is shunned like the plague as soon as no physical or other kind of coercion exists. External labor, the labor in which people alienate themselves, is a labor of self-sacrifice, of mortification. Finally, the externality of labor for the worker shows itself in the fact that it does not belong to him, but to someone else, that it is not his property, that in it he does not belong to himself, but to somebody else. As in religion the activity of human imagination, of the human brain and the human heart, works independently of the individual, *i.e.*, as an alien, divine or diabolical activity, so the worker's activity is not his own spontaneous doing. It belongs to someone else; it is the loss of his self.

As a result of this people (workers) feel themselves freely active only in their animal functions—eating, drinking, procreating—and beyond that at most with respect to their houses, dressing-up, etc. In their truly human functions they feel reduced to the level of animals. What is typical for animals becomes human, and what is human becomes reduced to animal functions.

Eating, drinking, and procreating are, to be sure, also genuine human functions. In the abstraction, however, in which they are divorced from the remaining context of human activities and in which they are made into sole and ultimate ends, they turn into animal functions.

We have considered the act of alienating practical human activity, work, with respect to two things: (1) The relation of the worker to the product of labor, to an alien object that has power over the worker. This relation is at the same time the relation to the sensuous external world, to the objects of nature as an alien world with a hostile disposition toward him. (2) The relation of labor to the act of production within work. This relation is the relation of the worker to his own activity as a strange activity not belonging to him, activity as suffering, strength as impotence, begetting as emasculation, the worker's own physical and mental energy, his personal life—what else is life but activity?—as an activity that is turned against him, which is independent of his will, and which in no way is his own. Alienation from one's self—as the alienation from objects mentioned above.

Now we have to deduce a third aspect of alienated labor from the two previous ones.

Man is a species being, not only by conceiving practically and theoretically of himself, as well as of other things, as a kind, but also—and this is only a different expression of the same thing—by relating to himself as the present, living kind, by relating to himself as a universal, and therefore free being.

*

By practically producing a world of objects, by transforming inorganic nature, man reveals himself as a conscious species being, *i.e.*, as a being that relates to his own kind of his own nature, or to himself as a species being. Animals, to be sure, produce as well. They build nests, dwellings, like the bees, beavers, ants, etc. But they produce only what they immediately need for themselves or their offspring; they produce one-sidedly, while humans produce universally. Animals produce only under the dominance of immediate physical needs, while humans produce even when free of such needs—indeed, humans produce in the proper sense only when they are free of them. Animals produce only themselves, while humans recreate the entire world. The animal's product belongs immediately to its physical body, while humans encounter their products in freedom. Animals perform only according to the needs of the species to which they belong while humans are capable of producing according to the needs of any species, and of applying everywhere the inherent standards to things. For this reason humans also produce according to the laws of beauty.

It is exactly in the transformation of the objective world that humans prove themselves to be species beings. This production is their active life as a species. Through it, nature appears as their work and reality. The object of labor is, therefore, the realization of the species life of humankind. In the object of labor man does not only look at himself intellectually, but practically—in a world created by himself. By robbing man of the object of his production, alienated labor robs him of his species life, his self-realization as a kind, and it turns his advantage over animals into the disadvantage of losing nature, his inorganic body.

Similarly, alienated labor, by degrading free, spontaneous activity to a means, turns the species life of humankind into the means for man's physical existence.

The consciousness that man has of his kind is changed through alienation in such a way that human life becomes a means.

Thus alienated labor turns:

(3) The species life of humanity, both nature and his spiritual capacity, into something that is alien to man, into a means of his individual existence. It alienates man from his own body, from external nature, from his spiritual nature, and from his humanity.

(4) An immediate consequence of the fact, that man is alienated from the product of his labor, from his life activity, and from the nature of his kind, is the alienation of man from man. When man encounters his self, he encounters the other man. What can be said about man's relation to his work, to the product of his labor, and to himself, can also be said about his relation to other men, as well as to their work and products.

In general, the statement that man is alienated from his species nature means that every man is alienated from every other man, and that every man is alienated from human nature.

The alienation of man (indeed, every relationship in which man stands to himself) only becomes real, *i.e.*, is expressed, in the relation in which man stands to other men.

Thus under the condition of alienated labor every individual views the other according to the standard and in proportion to his own existence as a worker.

We started with a fact of political economy, the alienation of the worker from his product. We have formulated the concept of this fact: estranged, alienated labor. We have analyzed this concept—thus merely showing the implications of a fact of political economy.

Let us now see how the concept of estranged, alienated labor represents itself in real life.

If the product of labor is alien to me, if I encounter it as an alien power, to whom, then, does it belong?

If my own activity does not belong to me, if it is an alien, forced activity, to whom does it belong?

To a being other than myself.

Who is this being?

The gods? It is true that in (the most) ancient times the major production, such as the construction of temples, etc., in Egypt, India, or Mexico, seemed to be for the benefit of the gods, and the gods seemed to be the owners of these products. However, the gods alone were never the lords of labor. No more than nature. And what a contradiction it would be if man were to renounce the joy of production and the enjoyment of the product in favour of gods and nature the more man subjugated nature by his labor and the more the miracles of the gods were rendered superfluous by the miracles of industry.

The alien being, to whom the process and product of labor belong, in whose service labor is performed and for whose benefit the product of labor is produced, can only be man.

Percy B. Shelley: "Song to the Men of England"

Shelley (1792-1822) is counted among the English writers of the Romantic period, but the anti-authoritarian radicalism of the Enlightenment is still a most important part of his work. Even as a young student he was influenced by such radical literature as William Godwin's Political Justice. *His views — highly unorthodox in the England of his time — brought him into endless conflicts with parents, schools, and courts. Disgusted with the social, political, and intellectual conditions at home, he spent the last years of his short life as an expatriate in Italy.*

"Song to the Men of England" (1818) addresses those whose hard work creates wealth, but who do not enjoy what they create. Shelley does not appeal to the mercy of philanthropists, but to the people who are the victims of their exploitative situation. He addresses them as men who actively create wealth, and who therefore should also liberate themselves from their misery. He addresses them, in other words, explicitly as beings who are capable of self-determination.

1

Men of England, wherefore plough
For the lords who lay ye low?
Wherefore weave with toil and care
The rich robes your tyrants wear?

2

Wherefore feed, and clothe, and save,
From the cradle to the grave,
Those ungrateful drones who would
Drain your sweat — nay, drink your blood!

3

Wherefore, Bees of England, forge
Many a weapon, chain, and scourge,
That these stingless drones may spoil
The forced produce of your toil?

4

Have ye leisure, comfort, calm,
Shelter, food, love's gentle balm?
Or what is it ye buy so dear
With your pain and with your fear?

5

The seed ye sow, another reaps;
The wealth ye find, another keeps;
The robes ye weave, another wears;
The arms ye forge, another bears.

6
Sow seed, — but let no tyrant reap;
Find wealth, — let no imposter heap;
Weave robes, — let not the idle wear;
Forge arms, — in your defense to bear.

7
Shrink to your cellars, holes, and cells;
In halls ye deck, another dwells.
Why shake the chains ye wrought? Ye see
The steel ye tempered glance on ye.

8
With plough and spade, and hoe and loom,
Trace your grave, and build your tomb,
And weave your winding-sheet, till fair
England be your sepulchre.

Heinrich Heine: "The Silesian Weavers"

Heine (1797-1856) was one of the most romantic, as well as one of the most critical and satirical German writers. He was born in the Rhineland, apprenticed in Hamburg, and then a student at several Universities. In the early thirties he left Germany with its backward and repressive social conditions and settled as a permanent exile in Paris. There he had contact with numerous ex-patriate writers and revolutionaries, who all used the relatively liberal conditions of the French capital to congregate and develop their ideas. Heine continued to write in German, becoming both a very popular writer whose lyrical poems became part of the German folk tradition, and a focus of hate for German conservatives who did not forgive him his derision of German political conditions (and who laid the groundwork for later anti-semitic campaigns against his work).

In 1844 the weavers of the Silesian cottage industry staged their famous hunger revolt, which was brutally suppressed. Heine published the following poem in the German exile newspaper Vorwärts:

No tears in their eyes,
they sit at their looms, grinding their teeth:
Germany, we are weaving your shroud!
And three curses we weave into it—
   We are weaving, we are weaving!

A curse on the God to whom we have prayed
in the winter's cold, and while without bread;
in vain we have waited and hoped.
He has mocked us, and fooled us, and lead us astray—
   We are weaving, we are weaving!

A curse on the King, the King of the rich,
whom our misery could not move,
who squeezes from us our very last dime,
and who has killed us like dogs—
   We are weaving, we are weaving!

A curse on the treacherous fatherland,
where only shame and dishonor can grow,
where every flower is nipped in the bud,
where rot and decay feed the worms—
   We are weaving, we are weaving!

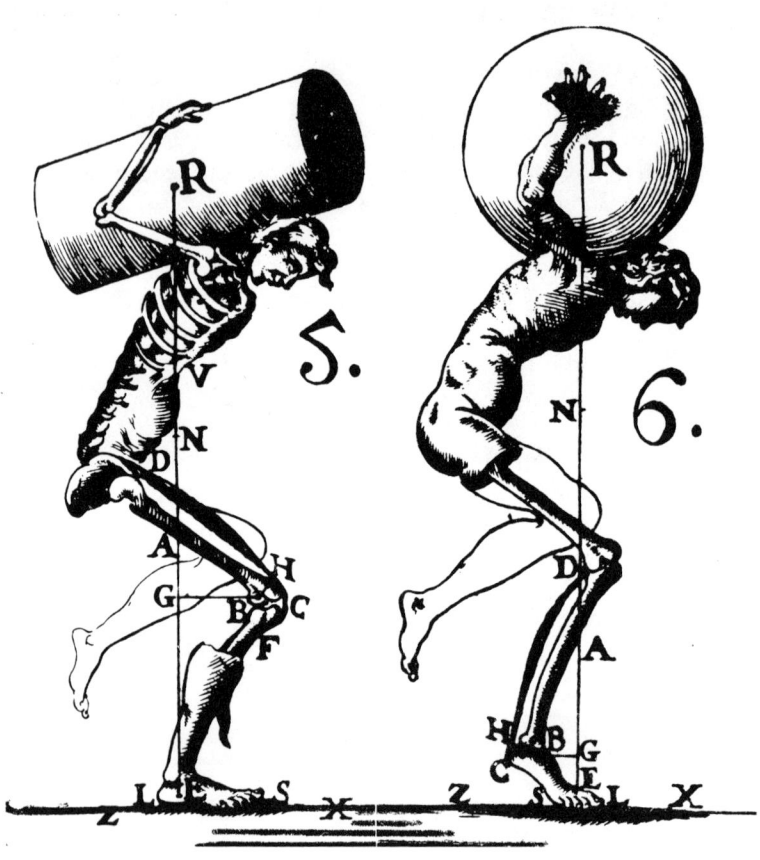

5. Man as Machine

VIII. THE SELF AS THE HIGHER HUMAN FACULTIES

SELF DETERMINATION

John S. Mill: *Utilitarianism*

AUTHOR AND TEXT: *Mill (1806-1873) was the most influential philosopher of the English speaking world in the nineteenth century, and he was the most capable and convincing defender of Utilitarianism, the philosophy which his father James Mill and Jeremy Bentham had developed. As an Empiricist in the British tradition, John Stuart Mill defended sense perception and empirical observation as the fundamental sources of human knowledge (thus opposing Kant and the other German Idealists who took innate reason to be the primary source of that knowledge). As a Utilitarian he defended Happiness as the highest principle of morality (again opposing the German Idealists who took Autonomy to be the highest value). Politically Mill was a Liberal, opposing the Conservatives to the right, but resisting also the radical Socialists to the left. In his famous book,* On Liberty *(1859) he argues for the rights of individuals and minorities in a democratic system of government. Encouraged by his congenial wife Harriet Taylor, he wrote a feminist tract,* The Subjection of Women *(1861, published 1869).*

The following text is the beginning of the second chapter of Utilitarianism *(1861).*

HAPPINESS AND SELF-REALIZATION: *In the following selection Mill defends the Happiness principle against the accusation that it will induce people to betray their proper human nature by reducing their aspirations to the level of animals. Against this Mill holds that human beings can only be really happy if they exert their specifically human capabilities, i.e., if they develop their lives beyond the gratification of their senses and material needs. Human happiness, in other words, may well imply, according to Mill, hard work, intellectual frustrations, sacrifice, and other things which usually are not counted among the desirable things in life. "It is better to be a human being dissatisfied than a pig satisfied; better to be Socrates dissatisfied than a fool satisfied," as he put it in his classical formulation. Human happiness, so Mill's contention, is different in kind from the happiness of animals.*

Utilitarianism has often been derided for its philistine shallowness by such thinkers as Dostoyevsky, Marx, and Nietzsche. The thinking of Thoreau and Emerson is also generally incompatible with the spirit of Utilitarianism. What the criticisms of these thinkers have in common is the conviction that the "avoidance of pain," one of the major points stressed by Utilitarians, will deprive people of their deepest insights into reality, and will prevent them from ever encountering their real selves. While this criticism may be valid with respect to many Utilitarians, such as Bentham and James Mill, John Stuart Mill's praise of the dissatisfied Socrates seems to concur with the conviction of the critics. If being condemned to death for one's unorthodox beliefs, as happened to Socrates, can be part of human happiness, then the difference between Utilitarians and their critics can ultimately not be very great.

The problem which arises for Mill is conceptual: If a life dominated by dissatisfaction, failure, frustrating work, and mortal danger can still be a "happy" life, then there may not be much point in declaring "happiness, and the "avoidance of pain" the basic principle of human behavior. In view of what such terms are to cover, "happiness" and "pain" may have become completely meaningless terms. It might have been better for Mill to have dropped them altogether, and to have described the goals of human endeavor in more concrete and specific terms. In this way it might have become clear immediately that Mill's type of Utilitarianism was not really incompatible with the views of his critics; much invective and useless argument might have been avoided.

~ ~ ~

A passing remark is all that needs be given to the ignorant blunder of supposing that those who stand up for utility as the test of right and wrong, use the term in that restricted and merely colloquial sense in which utility is opposed to pleasure. An apology is due to the philosophical opponents of ultilitarianism, for even the momentary appearance of confounding them with any one capable of so absurd a misconception; which is the more extraordinary, inasmuch as the contrary accusation, of referring everything to pleasure, and that too in its grossest form, is another of the common charges against utilitarianism; and, as has been pointedly remarked by an able writer, the same sort of persons, and often the very same persons, denounce the theory "as impracticably dry when the word utility precedes the word pleasure, and as too practicably voluptuous when the word pleasure precedes the word utility." Those who know anything about the matter are aware that every writer, from Epicurus to Bentham, who maintained the theory of utility, meant by it, not something to be contradistinguished from pleasure, but pleasure itself, together with exemption from pain; and instead of opposing the useful to the agreeable or the ornamental, have always declared that the useful means these, among other things. Yet the common herd, including the herd of writers, not only in newspapers and periodicals, but in books of weight and pretension, are perpetually falling into this shallow mistake. Having caught up the word utilitarian, while knowing nothing whatever about it but its sound, they habitually express by it the rejection, or the neglect, of pleasure in some of its forms; of beauty, of ornament, or of amusement. Nor is the term thus ignorantly misapplied solely in disparagement, but occasionally in compliment; as though it implied superiority to frivolity and the mere pleasures of the moment. And this perverted use is the only one in which the word is popularly known, and the one from which the new generation are acquiring their sole notion of its meaning. Those who introduced the word, but who had for many years discontinued it as a distinctive appellation, may well feel themselves called upon to resume it, if by doing so they can hope to contribute anything towards rescuing it from this utter degradation.

The creed which accepts as the foundation of morals, Utility, or the Greatest Happiness Principle, holds that actions are right in proportion as they tend to promote happiness, wrong as they tend to produce the reverse of happiness. By happiness is intended pleasure, and the absence of pain; by unhappiness, pain, and the privation of pleasure. To give a clear view of the moral standard set up by the theory, much more requires to be said; in particular, what things it includes in the ideas of pain and pleasure; and to what extent this is left an open question. But these supplementary explanations do not affect the theory of life on which this theory of morality is grounded,—namely, that pleasure, and freedom from pain, are the only things desirable as ends; and that all desirable things (which are as numerous in the utilitarian as in any other scheme) are desirable either for the pleasure inherent in themselves, or as means to the promotion of pleasure and the prevention of pain.

Now, such a theory of life excites in many minds, and among them in some of the most estimable in feeling and purpose, inveterate dislike. To suppose that life has (as they express it) no higher end than pleasure,—no better and nobler object of desire and pursuit,—they designate as utterly mean and grovelling; as a doctrine worthy only of swine, to whom the followers of Epicurus were, at a very early period, contemptuously likened; and modern holders of the doctrine are occasionally made the subject of equally polite comparisons by its German, French, and English assailants.

When thus attacked, the Epicureans have always answered, that it is not they, but their accusers, who represent human nature in a degrading light; since the accusation supposes human beings to be capable of no pleasures except those of which swine are capable. If this supposition were true, the charge could not be gainsaid, but would then be no longer an imputation; for if the sources of pleasure were precisely the same to human beings and to swine, the rule of life which is good enough for the one would be good enough for the other. The comparison of the Epicurean life to that of beasts is felt as degrading, precisely because a beast's pleasures do not satisfy a human being's conceptions of happiness. Human beings have faculties more elevated than the animal appetites, and when once made conscious of them, do not regard anything as happiness which does not include their gratification. I do not, indeed, consider the Epicureans to have been by any means faultless in drawing out their scheme of consequences from the utilitarian principle. To do this in any sufficient manner, many Stoic, as well as Christian elements require to be included. But there is no known Epicurean theory of life which does not assign to the pleasures of the intellect, of the feelings and imagination, and of the moral sentiments, a much higher value as pleasures than to those of mere sensation. It must be admitted, however, that utilitarian writers in general have placed the superiority of mental over bodily pleasures chiefly in the greater permanency, safety, uncostliness, etc., of the former, — that is, in their circumstantial advantages rather than in their intrinsic nature. And on all these points utilitarians have fully proved their case; but they might have taken the other, and, as it may be called, higher ground, with entire consistency. It is quite compatible with the principle of utility to recognize the fact, that some *kinds* of pleasure are more desirable and more valuable than others. It would be absurd that while, in estimating all other things, quality is considered as well as quantity, the estimation of pleasure should be supposed to depend on quantity alone.

If I am asked what I mean by difference of quality in pleasures, or what makes one pleasure more valuable than another, merely as a pleasure, except its being greater in amount, there is but one possible answer. Of two pleasures, if there be one to which all or almost all who have experience of both give a decided preference, irrespective of any feeling of moral obligation to prefer it, that is the more desirable pleasure. If one of the two is, by those who are competently acquainted with both, placed so far above the other that they prefer it, even though knowing it to be attended with a greater amount of discontent, and would not resign it for any quantity of the other pleasure which their nature is capable of, we are justified in ascribing to the preferred enjoyment a superiority in quality, so far outweighing quantity as to render it, in comparison, of small account.

Now it is an unquestionable fact that those who are equally acquainted with, and equally capable of appreciating and enjoying both, do give a most marked preference to the manner of existence which employs their higher faculties. Few human creatures would consent to be changed into any of the lower animals, for a promise of the fullest allowance of a beast's pleasures; no intelligent human being would consent to be a fool, no instructed person would be an ignoramus, no person of feeling and conscience would be selfish and base, even though they should be persuaded that the fool, the dunce, or the rascal is better satisfied with his lot than they are with theirs. They would not resign what they possess more than he, for the most complete satisfaction of all the desires which they have in common with him. If they ever fancy they would, it is only in cases of unhappiness so extreme, that to escape from it they would exchange their lot for almost any other, however undesirable in their own eyes. A being of higher faculties requires more to make him happy, is capable probably of more acute suffering, and is certainly accessible to it at more points, than one of an inferior type; but in spite of these liabilities, he can never really wish to sink into what he feels to be a lower grade of existence. We may give what explanation we please of this unwillingness; we may attribute it to pride, a name which is given indiscriminately to some of the most and to some of the least estimable feelings of which mankind are capable; we may refer it to the love of liberty and personal independence, an appeal to which was with the Stoics one of the most effective means for the inculcation of it; to the love of power, or to the love of excitement, both of which do really enter into and contribute to it; but its most appropriate appellation is a sense of dignity, which all human beings possess in one form or other, and in some, though by no means in exact proportion to their higher faculties, and which is so essential a part of the happiness of those in whom it is strong, that nothing which conflicts with it could be, otherwise than momentarily, an object of desire to them. Whoever supposes that this preference takes place at a sacrifice of happiness—that the superior being, in anything like equal circumstances, is not happier than the inferior—confounds the two very different ideas, of happiness, and content. It is indisputable that the being whose capacities of enjoyment are low, has the greatest chance of having them fully satisfied; and a highly endowed being will always feel that any happiness which he can look for, as the world is constituted, is imperfect. But he can learn to bear its imperfections, if they are at all bearable; and they will not make him envy the being who is indeed unconscious of the imperfections, but only because he feels not at all the good which those imperfections qualify. It is better to be a human being dissatisfied than a pig satisfied; better to be Socrates dissatisfied than a fool satisfied. And if the fool, or the pig, is of a different opinion, it is because they only know their own side of the question. The other party to the comparison knows both sides.

It may be objected, that many who are capable of the higher pleasures, occasionally, under the influence of temptation, postpone them to the lower. But this is quite compatible with a full appreciation of the intrinsic superiority of the higher. Men often, from infirmity of character, make their election for the nearer good, though they know it to be the less valuable; and this no less when the choice is between two bodily pleasures, than when it is between bodily and mental. They pursue sensual indulgences to the injury of health, though perfectly aware that health is the greater good. It may be further objected, that many who begin with youthful enthusiasm for everything noble, as they advance in years sink into indolence and selfishness. But I do not believe that those who undergo this very common change, voluntarily choose the lower description of pleasures in preference to the higher. I believe that before they devote themselves exclusively to the one, they have already become incapable of the other. Capacity for the nobler feelings is in most natures a very tender plant, easily killed, not only by hostile influences, but by mere want of sustenance; and in the majority of young persons it speedily dies away if the occupations to which their position in life has devoted them, and the society into which it has thrown them, are not favorable to keeping that higher capacity in exercise. Men lose their high aspirations as they lose their intellectual tastes, because they have not time or opportunity for indulging them; and they addict themselves to inferior pleasures, not because they deliberately prefer them, but because they are either the only ones to which they have access, or the only ones which they are any longer capable of enjoying. It may be questioned whether any one who has remained equally susceptible to both classes of pleasures, ever knowingly and calmly preferred the lower; though many, in all ages, have broken down in an ineffectual attempt to combine both.

From this verdict of the only competent judges, I apprehend there can be no appeal. On a question which is the best worth having of two pleasures, or which of two modes of existence is the most grateful to the feelings, apart from its moral attributes and from its consequences, the judgment of those who are qualified by knowledge of both, or, if they differ, that of the majority among them, must be admitted as final. And there needs be the less hesitation to accept this judgment respecting the quality of pleasures, since there is no other tribunal to be referred to even on the question of quantity. What means are there of determining which is the acutest of two pains, or the intensest of two pleasurable sensations, except that general suffrage of those who are familiar with both? Neither pains not pleasures are homogeneous, and pain is always heterogeneous with pleasure. What is there to decide whether a particular pleasure is worth purchasing at the cost of a particular pain, except the feelings and judgment of the experienced? When, therefore, those feelings and judgment declare the pleasures derived from the higher faculties to be preferable *in kind*, apart from the question of intensity, to those of which the animal nature, disjoined from the higher faculties, is susceptible, they are entitled on this subject to the same regard.

A Satirical Poem From *Punch*

Mill's discussion raises the question of what kind of being humans are: sensuous creatures who are basically out for material consumption and survival, or spiritual beings who are destined to transcend the animalistic aspects of their existence. This question became prominent in the intellectual turmoil surrounding the Theory of Evolution. In 1844 Robert Chambers suggested in his Vestiges of the Natural History of Creation *that man had descended from a monkey, or that both had a common ancestor. In 1852 Herbert Spencer's* The Development Hypothesis *appeared, which started a whole school of thought and a worldview centered around the idea of the "survival of the fittest." Charles Darwin's* On the Origin of Species *(1859) gave considerable scientific support to the idea of the evolution of humans from the lower animal species. For many people the idea of Evolution provoked an ideological crisis of identity. They felt that humans could not be considered spiritual beings if it were true that they had evolved from lower animals, instead of being created in a different act which would radically separate them from the animal kingdom. This question of the true human identity is humorously taken up by the following poem from the British satirical magazine Punch:*

>The *Vestiges* taught
>That all come from naught
>By "development" so called "progressive",
>That insects and worms
>Assume higher forms
>By modification excessive.
>
>Then Darwin set forth
>In a book of much worth
>The importance of "Nature's selection",
>How the struggle for life
>Is a laudable strife
>And results in "specific distinction".
>
>Am I satyr or man?
>Pray tell me who can,
>And settle my place in the scale,
>A man in ape's shape,
>An anthropoid ape,
>Or a monkey deprived of its tail?

Charles Baudelaire: "The Ideal"

Emphasis on what is "higher" has always played an important part in Western culture—a fact which has to do with the dominant definition of man as a spiritual being. While this emphasis was more often than not a mere wish or pretense, it has also inspired people to transcend the inherent limitations of the animal world, or the narrow-mindedness, triviality, or corruption of everyday life in society. Even at times when religion was clearly on the defensive, philosophers and poets often expressed a longing for a different kind of existence than the one they were involved in. In the poem "Elevation," Charles Baudelaire (1821-1867) suggests such a flight of the mind:

> High above the quiet lakes and valleys,
> High above mountains, woods, the seas and clouds,
> Beyond the glowing sun, beyond the ether,
> Beyond the spheres of stars
> You move, my spirit, with agility, . . .

This kind of idealism was always in danger of losing touch with reality, with the material base of life, and to degenerate into empty verbiage and dishonest posturing. Partly in response to such posturing, many writers of the nineteenth century turned to crude forms of materialism. (Cf., e.g., Robert Büchner's slogan "Der Mensch ist was er isst"—"Man is what he eats.") Generally thinkers became aware of how vague and ungrounded spiritualistic theories become unless they are rooted in identifiable, down-to-earth experiences. Thus many writers began to turn their attention to the "unofficial" aspects of society, to the mysteries of the body, and to the dark part of the soul that Freud was to call the Unconscious. Nietzsche, e.g., wrote: "But it is with man as it is with the tree. The more he aspires to the height and light, the more strongly do his roots strive earthward, downward, into the dark, the deep—into evil." (It need not be mentioned that to the Victorian mind the repressed aspects of life easily connoted "evil.")

Baudelaire's collection of poems, The Flowers of Evil, *has to be seen in this context. (The book appeared in 1857, and was immediately condemned by the French courts as a violation of public morality—just as Gustave Flaubert's* Madame Bovary, *which appeared in the same year.) In his poems Baudelaire developed spiritual sublimation to an extreme, but he also delved into depths of lust and suffering which had rarely been reached before by a writer. In "The Ideal" he flies into the face of what was considered ideal and cultured by most of his contemporaries. By praising the murderous Lady Macbeth, the stories of infidelity, incest, patricide, and power struggles of Aeschylus, and the far from "feminine" sculpture of the woman representing* Night *by Michelangelo, Baudelaire praises the reckless strength and vitality of overpowering characters, rather than the ethereal goodness that appealed to the Victorians. The "red ideal" of Baudelaire is clearly one of revolt:*

> It will never be the vignettes' beauty,
> The shallow products of weak times,
> (Those dainty feet with slippers, those fingers with the castanets)
> Which will satisfy a heart like mine.
>
> Gavarni you can have, that poet of the sick,
> His chatting swarms of beauties from the hospital,
> For I can't find among those roses without color
> A flower like my red ideal.
>
> What's missing in my heart—deep like an abyss—
> Is you, Lady Macbeth, a powerful soul in crime,
> The dream of Aeschylus surfacing in the North;
>
> Or also you, great Night, daughter of Michelangelo,
> Who quietly, in a strange pose, shows all
> The ecstasies made for the Titans' mouths.

6. Man-Made World

IX. THE SELF AS NOTHING

SELF DETERMINATION

Fyodor Dostoyevsky: *Notes From Underground*

AUTHOR AND TEXT: *Dostoyevsky (1821-1881) very early became aware of the social conditions in Czarist Russia — absolute monarchy, serfdom, conservativism of the Orthodox Church, and oppressive bureaucracy. In 1839 Dostoyevsky's father was murdered by his serfs, whom he had treated with utter brutality. In the late forties, when revolutions were impending everywhere in Europe, Dostoyevsky joined a number of revolutionary groups. In 1849 he was arrested and sentenced to death. While in front of the firing squad, he and his comrades were given a last minute reprieve. His next nine years were spent in Siberia, first as a prisoner, then as a private in the army.*

Dostoyevsky's views changed fundamentally toward the end of his life, when new revolutionary groups were forming in Russia; he then had become one of the most conservative writers in his country and an ardent defender of Czardom. He went so far as to argue that only the hegemony of Russia and the Orthodox Church over Europe could lead to acceptable social conditions. The ideas of the Enlightenment were the major target of his criticisms. His colleague Turgenev called him "the most malignant Christian" he had ever met.

The root of Dostoyevsky's conservatism was his growing conviction that humankind was fundamentally and hopelessly evil. In the light of this conviction the optimism of the Enlightenment, with its goal of the general emancipation of humanity, looked foolish and superficial. It was this pessimism which began to emerge in Dostoyevsky's Notes From Underground *(1864). The story portrays a nameless city dweller who is cut off from all ties to community and tradition, but who also cannot find anything but pain, confusion, emptiness and despair in himself. He is a man for whom there is no center in his life, no point of hold and orientation — neither in the external, nor in the inner world. In the course of the story this negative hero reveals the most pitiful and ugly thoughts and feelings — with a candor and realism which hardly any writer had previously achieved. Yet,*

The Self As Nothing

the narrator also suggests that these embarrassing confessions do not describe the full depth of degradation in which the protagonist (together with the rest of humanity) finds himself. The truth is that the human soul is a bottomless abyss. — It was this extreme experience of social isolation and self-loss which made the Underground Man a forerunner of the anti-hero in twentieth century Existentialism.

The following excerpts have been translated by James Hadra.

~ ~ ~

I admit that reason is a good thing. You can't argue about that. But reason is just reason and it only satisfies your rational requirements. Desire, however, is the manifestation of life itself, all of life, encompassing everything from reason right down to scratching an itch. And even then, when we're guided by our desires, life may still turn out to be a messy affair. But it's still life and not some series of extractions of square roots.

Take me, for example. I instinctively want to live to exercise every aspect of life in me, not just reason which is only about one-twentieth of the whole.

And what does reason know? It only know what it has had time to learn. There are many things which it will never know. That's not very encouraging but it has to be said.

Now human nature is quite the opposite. It acts as an entity. It uses everything it has, conscious and unconscious, and even if it deceives us, it is alive. I suspect, ladies and gentlemen, that you regard me with pity, and wonder just how I can fail to understand that an enlightened, cultured man, the man of the future, could not deliberately wish to harm himself. It's just mathematics to you. I agree, it is mathematics. But I must repeat for the hundredth time that there is one instance when a man can, fully aware, wish upon himself something harmful, stupid or even just plain idiotic. He will do it in order to establish his right to wish for even the most idiotic things and not be required to have only sensible wishes. But what if some really absurd whim, my friends, turns out to be the most advantageous thing of all for us? It sometimes happens. Specifically, it may be more advantageous to us than all other advantages even if it obviously does us harm and goes against all sensible conclusions of our reason concerning our self-interest, because, whatever else, it leaves us our one most important, most treasured possession: our own individuality.

Some people will concede, for example, that desire may well be the thing man treasures most. Desire can, if it wishes, of course, agree with reason, particularly if it is used sparingly, never going too far. Then desire is quite useful, even worthy of praise.

But in reality, desire is usually stubborn in its disagreement with reason and . . . and . . . I must say that is also useful and praiseworthy.

Let's assume, friends, that man isn't stupid. (Indeed, if we say he is stupid, then whom could we call intelligent?) But even if he isn't stupid, he is still monstrously ungrateful. Incredibly so! I would even go so far as to say that man is best defined as: ungrateful biped. But even this is not his main defect. His main defect is chronic perverseness, an affliction he has suffered from throughout his history, from the Flood down to the crisis of Schleswig-Holstein. Perverseness is due to lack of common sense. Just take a look at the history of mankind and tell me what your see. Do you find it grand? Perhaps so. The Colossus of Rhodes is so impressive that it prompted Mr. Anayavsky to say that some consider it a creation of nature. Do you find it colorful? Yes, I guess there's plenty of color throughout human history. Just think about all the military dress uniforms and the formal civilian dress. That's quite impressive in itself. And if we think of all the uniforms worn on semi-official occasions, then there's so much color that any historian has to be dazzled by it. Do you find it monotonous? Yes, you do have a good point there. They fight, fight, fight; they are fighting now, they've fought before and they'll fight again in the future. Yes, I agree it's just a bit too monotonous.

So you see, you can say just anything about world history; anything and everything that the most morbid imagination can think up. Except for one thing, of course. You can't say that world history is reasonable. The word sticks in your throat. And here's what happens all the time: good, reasonable men, wise men, humanitarians, try to live consistently good and sensible lives serving, as one might say, as human beacons lighting the way for their neighbors, to prove to them that it can be done. And what comes of it? Sure enough, sooner or later, these lovers of mankind just give up, some in the midst of a scandal, often quite a messy one, too.

Now, let me ask you something: what can you expect from man, considering that he's such a strange creature? You can shower upon him all earthly blessings, drown him in happiness so that nothing can be seen but bubbles rising to the surface of his bliss, make him economically so secure that he won't have anything to do but sleep, munch cakes, and worry about keeping world history flowing . . . and even then, out of sheer spite and ingratitude, he will still play a dirty trick on you. He'll even risk the cake for the sake of some glaring stupidity, some economically unsound nonsense, just to inject into all the soundness and sense around him some of his own disastrous, fatal fancies. What he wants to preserve is precisely those noxious fancies of his, those vulgar trivialities, if only to assure himself that men are still men (as if that were so important) and not piano keys simply responding to the laws of nature. Man is somehow averse to the idea of not being able to desire unless the desire happens to fit into his timetable of the moment.

But even if man were just a piano key, even if this could be mathematically demonstrated to him . . . even then, he wouldn't come to his senses, even then he'd pull some trick out of his sheer ingratitude just to make his point. And even if he didn't have them ready at hand, he'd devise some means of destruction, chaos, and all sorts of suffering to clutter his way. For instance, he'd swear loud enough for the whole world to hear—swearing is the prerogative of man which sets him apart from the other animals—and just maybe his swearing alone might get him what he wanted, I mean, it would prove to him that he's a man and not just a piano key.

Now you may say that even this can be calculated in advance and put into the timetable, the chaos, the swearing and everything, and that the very possibility of such calculation would prevent it, and that thus sanity would prevail. Oh no! If that were the case, man would go insane on purpose, just to be immune from reason. I believe this is so and I will vouch for it, because it seems to me that the meaning of man's life consists in proving to himself over and again that he's a man and not just a piano key. And he will keep on proving it and paying for it with his own skin; he'll even become a troglodyte if necessary. And since this is so, I can't help but rejoice that things are still the way they are and that, at least for now, nobody knows a snippet about what determines our desires.

Now you may shout that no one intends to deprive me of my free will, that they are only trying to arrange things so that my will coincides with what is in my own best interest, the laws of nature, and mathematics.

Ah, my friends, don't give me any talk about free will when it comes to timetables and mathematics, when everything will be deducible from the old two-plus-two-makes-four! There's no need for free will to find out that two twice equals four. That's not what I call free will!

*

Of course I'm joking, friends, and I'm aware my jokes are weak ones. Yet, everything can't be simply laughed off. Perhaps my jokes are through clenched teeth. You see, certain questions haunt me, and perhaps you'll permit me to ask them.

Now you, for instance, — you want to cure man of his old bad habits and reshape his will according to the requirements of science and common sense. But why do you think man can or *should* be changed in such a way? What leads you to conclude that it is absolutely necessary to change man's desires? How do you know that these "corrections" will really be to man's advantage? And, if you'll permit me to be quite frank about it, what is it that makes you so sure that refraining from acting against one's interests, as determined by reason and mathematics, is always to one's advantage and that this is applicable to mankind as a whole?

So far, these are nothing but assumptions on your part. I'll concede that they conform to the laws of logic, but do they conform to human law? Before you call me crazy, let me explain. I'll agree that man is a creative animal that is doomed to strive consciously toward a goal, engaged in full-time engineering, so to speak, building himself roads that must lead *somewhere*—it doesn't matter where. And maybe if now and then he feels like straying, it's because he is *doomed* to build that road; even the man of action, stupid as he may be, has to realize from time to time that his road always goes *somewhere* and that the main thing is not *where* it goes, but just making sure the well-meaning fellow keeps at his engineering tasks, and away from the deadly traps of idleness, which, as we all know, is the mother of all vice. There's no arguing that man likes to create and to build roads. But why does he also like chaos and disorder even into old age? Just explain that, if you can! But wait, I also have a few words to say on this subject. I wonder if perhaps he doesn't like chaos and destructiveness so much because, instinctively, he's afraid of reaching the goal he's set for himself. How do you know? Perhaps he likes his goal only from a distance; perhaps he only likes to contemplate it, not live with it, preferring to leave it, when he gets right down to it, to animals, ants, sheep and so on. Of course, ants are different. They have the most wonderful everlasting piece of engineering to work on: the anthill.

The worthy ants began with their own anthill and will probably end up with it, which is highly to the credit of their single-mindedness and perseverance. But man, frivolous and unaccountable, rather like a chess player perhaps, enjoys the achieving rather than the goal itself.

Who can tell? Perhaps man's purpose in life on earth lies precisely in this continuous striving for a goal. That is, the purpose is life itself and not the goal, which must be, of course, two-plus-two-makes-four. And two-plus-two, my friends, is no longer life, but the beginning of death. At least man has always feared this two-plus-two-makes-four and it's what I'm afraid of now.

Let's assume that man does nothing but search for this two-plus-two, that he crosses oceans and sacrifices his very life in the quest, all the time fearing to find it does make four. He feels that once he has found it out, there'll be nothing left for him to search for. Workers, at least, when they get their wages at the end of the week, go to some tavern and then, maybe, wind up at the police station, so there's *something* to keep them busy. But otherwise, what's a man to do with himself when he reaches one of his goals? In any case, he is visibly awkward whenever he does. He loves the achieving, but doesn't particularly enjoy what he achieves. That's funny, isn't it? Yes, man is a comical animal, and there's clearly a joke in all this. But I still say that two-plus-two is an unbearable notion, an arrogant imposition. This two-plus-two image stands there with its hands in its pockets, right in the middle of your road, and spits in your direction. Nonetheless, I'm willing to agree the two-plus-two-makes-four is a thing of beauty. But if we're going to praise everything like that, then I will say that two-plus-two-makes-five is also a delightful little item once in a while.

And what makes you so sure, so positive that only the normal, the positive, *i.e.*, only what promotes man's welfare, is to his advantage? Can't reason also be wrong as to what's an advantage? Why can't man like things besides his well-being? Maybe suffering pleases him just as much. Maybe suffering is just as much an advantage to him as well-being. In truth, man adores suffering. Passionately. And that's a fact. For this you don't even have to go to world history. Just ask yourself, if you've had any kind of experience of life. And I even feel, personally, that it's shameful to like well-being just in itself. Right or wrong, it's really pleasant to break something once in a while.

Really, I'm not advocating suffering over well-being. What I'm for is whim, and I want the right to use it whenever I want to.

I know, for example, that suffering is inadmissible in light stage plays. In the Utopian Crystal Palace it would be inconceivable, because suffering means doubt and denial, and what kind of a Crystal Palace would that turn out to be, if one had doubts about it? Nonetheless, I'm convinced that man will never give up true suffering, that is, chaos and destructiveness. After all, suffering is the only source of consciousness. And even though I stated at the outset that consciousness is man's greatest plague, I do know he likes it and won't exchange it for any advantage. Consciousness, for instance, is of a much higher order than two-plus-two. After two-plus-two, of course, we'll have nothing left to do or to find out. All we'll have left to use is to block out our five senses and plunge into contemplation. Even with consciousness we haven't much to do either, but at least we can lacerate ourselves once in a while, and that does liven us up a little. I may go against progress, but it's better than nothing.

Matthew Arnold: "Dover Beach"

Arnold (1822-1888) lived a relatively quiet life. He made a living as a college teacher, and as an inspector of schools. His view of his contemporaries, however, was not gentle. England, according to him, was populated by barbarians, philistines, and an uninspired mass lacking all standards and direction. His view of the world, in fact, was one of darkness, joylessness, and pain. Like Dostoyevsky's Underground Man he realized that the old world with its faith, standards, and order had essentially vanished. And in its place he did not find liberty and an emancipated humanity, but chaos, emptiness, and degradation. This outlook brings Arnold, as Dostoyevsky, close to the experience of the world which in the twentieth century was to shape the thoughts and feelings of the Existentialists.

"Dover Beach" begins with the description of an enchanted night at the seashore, a world "which seems to lie

before us like a land of dreams." But this calm and beauty is illusory. The poet's reflections turn to the actual state of the world, the wars, the coldness of social relations, the pain — and in the light of these the world appears to him like a *"plain, swept with confused alarms of struggle and flight, where ignorant armies clash by night."* The poem mentions that once the world had been a wholesome place, namely when "faith" gave order and direction to everyone's life, when things were held together by a common and comprehensive view and purpose. But that faith is dead: traditional religion is out of step with the actual development of culture. Thus, only the "naked," purposeless, and disconnected facts of history are left, a lightless, cold, and utterly desolate world.

It is this desperate, inhospitable state of the world which is the motivating force that draws two lovers together. Because there is no satisfaction or consolation in the world, the beloved person has to be everything. The love of such a modern couple can no longer come out of the strength and attraction of the individuals, but is largely inspired by the dreadfulness of the world. This love gains its melancholy fascination and intensity solely before the background of a dark and disenchanted world.

> The sea is calm tonight,
> The tide is full, the moon lies fair
> Upon the straits; — on the French coast the light
> Gleams and is gone; the cliffs of England stand,
> Glimmering and vast, out in the tranquil bay.
> Come to the window, sweet is the night-air!
> Only, from the long line of spray
> Where the sea meets the moon-blanched land,
> Listen! you hear the grating roar
> Of pebbles which the waves draw back, and
>   fling,
> At their return, up the high strand,
> Begin, and cease, and then again begin,
> With tremulous cadence slow, and bring
> The eternal note of sadness in.

Sophocles long ago
Heard it on the Aegaean, and it brought
Into his mind the turbid ebb and flow
Of human misery; we
Find also in the sound a thought,
Hearing it by this distant northern sea.

The Sea of Faith
Was once, too, at the full, and round earth's shore
Lay like the folds of a bright girdle furled.
But now I only hear
Its melancholy, long, withdrawing roar,
Retreating, to the breath
Of the night-wind, down the vast edges drear
And naked shingles of the world.

Ah, love, let us be true
To one another! for the world, which seems
To lie before us like a land of dreams,
So various, so beautiful, so new,
Hath really neither joy, nor love, nor light,
Nor certitude, nor peace, nor help for pain;
And we are here as on a darkling plain
Swept with confused alarms of struggle and flight,
Where ignorant armies clash by night.

Emily Dickinson: "I Heard A Fly Buzz When I Died"

This poem (probably written in 1862) is stunningly modern because of its untraditional perspective (a person recording her or his own death), and because of its seemingly irreverent focus on something mundane like a fly, while death is approaching. It seems incongruous that a fly should command so much attention in a situation where a whole existence is coming to an end.

The juxtaposition of a very important and a very unimportant event, the dying and the fly's buzz, is, of course, the point of the poem. The perspective on things which makes a fly and the dying equals, passes a certain judgment on the world. While making the buzzing fly more important than it seems to the ordinary consciousness, it degrades the circumstances of dying (the witnesses and what goes with them) in a way that would ordinarily be perceived as shockingly disrespectful. Dying makes all the things of the world insignificant, particularly the social matters which usually dominate people's minds. This is expressed in the poem by the dying person's mentioning that there is an "assignable" part of her or him, and another one that remains after the former has been willed to the world. For the non-"assignable" part of the dying person the witnesses and their worldly affairs recede into the background, while the fly becomes the main object of attention—until it, too, vanishes in the failing light.

What is important in the poem is its perspective. The view of the world of a dying person is to reveal something significant about the world. The significant insight is that all things are radically equal, that there is no such thing as an inherently important or unimportant object or state of affairs. The hierarchies of values which for ordinary consciousness orders the things of the world according to their assumed importance is a mere projection of people's minds. They are an illusion which is created and reinforced by the conduct of everyday life, by the relationships in which people stand to each other while living in society. A dying person who leaves all this will look through this illusion and see things in their plainness—their "nakedness," as Arnold said in "Dover Beach." And seeing the world naked is to see that ultimately it has no inherent structure, no inherent hierarchy of values, or any fixed proportions—that it consists of just so many facts without particular significance. Thus, the quiet poem by Dickinson suggests the same view of the world as the more dramatic one by Arnold. In an inconspicuous way it foreshadows the kind of metaphysical desolation which was to dominate much of twentieth century literature.

The Self as Nothing

I heard a fly buzz when I died —
The stillness in the room
Was like the stillness in the air
Between the heaves of storm.

The eyes around had wrung them dry
And breaths were gathering form
For that last onset when the King
Be witnessed in the room.

I willed my keepsakes, signed away
What portion of me be
Assignable — and then it was
There interposed a fly,

With blue, uncertain, stumbling buzz,
Between the light and me.
And then the windows failed, and then
I could not see to see.

7. Body and Mind

X. The Self as Body

Friedrich Nietzsche: "Of The Despisers Of The Body", et al.

AUTHOR AND TEXT: *Friedrich Nietzsche (1844-1900) is one of those writers who is largely ignored by academic philosophers because he is too literary, and who is ignored by writers and academic critics because he is too philosophical. Nietzsche's work, in other words, defies the usual academic division of labor. Yet, Nietzsche was one of the most profound and brilliant forerunners of such contemporary movements as Psychoanalysis and Existentialism, and one of the most penetrating critics of Western Civilization. His insights inspired scores of twentieth century intellectuals—including those who misunderstood his work as a proto-fascist doctrine. Nietzsche refused to construct a philosophical "system," arguing that individual, seemingly disconnected analyses, expressed in short, well-written aphorisms are more honest and insightful than lengthy, scholarly treatises which tend to bend everything to fit a pre-conceived theory. (Thus, his writings are, on occasion, self-contradictory. The way to read Nietzsche is not to figure out how the many things he wrote can be fit into one abstract formula, but to consider every piece as an experiment which either succeeds or fails in itself.) The complacency of the civilization which Nietzsche criticized so mercilessly made any success in his lifetime impossible. Nietzsche became a celebrity during the time when the pretenses of European culture headed for their first massive breakdown, at the time of World War I.*

MIND AND BODY: *The predominant traditional view in Western philosophy has always been that human beings have a two-fold nature, namely mind and body, and that there is a constant struggle between the two, ideally resulting in the dominance of the mind over the body. In this view mind and body are thought of as two independent agents or centers. It is this assumption which Nietzsche calls childish. The mature view, according to him, would be to recognize that the mind is only an aspect of the body, one of its many organs, and thoroughly under its control. Consequently, when there is a struggle "between mind and body," the body is really struggling* *against itself. When certain Christians, e.g., try to mortify their flesh, then this is merely a sign that the body is divided against itself, that the body wants to go under.*

OVER-MAN: *This is one of Nietzsche's most popularized terms. The German word is "Übermensch," and it used to be translated as "Superman." The "Übermensch" envisaged by Nietzsche does not even remotely resemble the famous cartoon character, and there is also no hint in the German word that such a person has to be male. An "over-man" would be someone who makes extraordinary demands on himself or herself, and who acquires a high degree of mastery over everything, including one's own personality. Wild passions and the "flesh," however, are not mortified, but used creatively (in the way in which a good rider will not beat a spirited horse into a submissive creature, but learn how to ride it by taking chances). The over-man affirms life while keenly aware of its terrors. The highest goal is not painless happiness, but intensity of every experience, whether joyful or hard.*

~ ~ ~

I want to speak my words to the despisers of the body. I do not want them to reform their studies and their teachings. I only want them to say farewell to their own body — and thus to be quiet.

"I am body and soul" — that is what a child would say. And why shouldn't one talk like a child?

But the adult, the knowledgeable says: I am body through and through, and nothing beside it; and soul is nothing but a word for something belonging to the body.

The body is one great reason, a variety with one sense, a war and a peace, a herd and a herder.

A tool of your body is also your little reason, my brother, which you call "spirit," a little tool and toy of your great reason.

"I" you say, and you are proud of the word. But the greater is — which you do not want to believe — your body and its great reason. This reason does not say I, but it does I.

What your sense feels and what your mind recognizes never has an end in itself. But sense and mind want to persuade you that they are the end of everything — that's how vain they are.

Tool and toy are sense and mind: beyond them there is still the self. The self also searches with the eyes of the senses, it also listens with the ears of the mind.

The self is always listening and always searching: it compares, subjects, conquers, destroys. It rules, and it also dominates the I.

Behind your thoughts and feelings, my brother, stands a powerful ruler, an unknown sage — he is called the self. In your body he resides; he is your body.

There is more reason in your body than in your best wisdom. And who knows to what end your body needs your best wisdom?

Your self laughs at your ego and its proud jumps. "What are these jumps and flights of thought to me?" it says to itself. "A detour to my end. I am the leash of the ego, and the inspirator of its notions."

The self says to the ego: "There, feel pain!" And then the ego suffers and thinks how the suffering could be stopped — and that's exactly why it *ought* to think.

The self says to the ego: "There, feel pleasure!" And then the ego feels delight and thinks how it could do so more often — and that is why it *ought* to think.

I want to say this to the despisers of the body: the fact that they despise shows that they respect. But what brought about this despising and respecting?

The creative self brought about respect and despising for its own sake, it created ecstasy and pain. The creative body produced the spirit as a hand of its will.

Even in your foolishness and contempt, you despisers of the body, you are the servants of your self. I say unto you: your self itself wants to die and turns its back to life.

It is not capable anymore of doing what it would like to do most: to create over and above itself. That is what it would like most, that is its innermost desire.

But for that it is too late now — thus your self wants to go under, you despisers of the body.

Your self wants to go under, and that is why you became despisers of the body! For you are not capable anymore to be creative over and above yourselves.

And therefore you are irritated at life and the earth. An unrecognized envy resides in the malevolent glances of your contempt.

I do not travel your road, despisers of the body! You are no bridges to Over-man!

Thus spoke Zarathustra.

Thus Spoke Zarathustra

They despised the body: they did not take it into account. Not only that: they treated it like an enemy. Their delusion was to believe that one could carry around a "beautiful soul" in a crippled cadaver . . . In order to make this plausible also to others they found it necessary to conceive of the idea of a "beautiful soul" in a different way, to revaluate the natural value, until finally a pale, sickly, idiotic-fanciful person could be perceived as perfection, as "angel-like," as transfiguration, as a higher human being.

The Will To Power

... Many hidden places and heights in the landscape around Nice have become sacred to me through unforgettable moments; the decisive section which is called "Of Old and New Tablets" I composed while making the difficult ascent from the station to the wonderful moorish cliff dwelling of Eza. My muscle flexibility was always at its peak when my creative power flew most abundantly. The *body* is inspired; let's leave the "soul" out of this . . . Often people could see me dance; in those days I could hike seven, eight hours across the mountains without even thinking of tiredness. I slept well, I laughed a lot—I was perfectly vigorous and patient.

Ecce Homo

Whoever has even a rough idea of the body—of its many simultaneously working systems, of its many cooperative and conflicting activities, of the delicacy of its balances, etc.—will judge that all consciousness is, by comparison, something poor and narrow; he will judge that no mind will even remotely be adequate for that which the mind would have to do here, and perhaps that the wisest teacher of morality and legislator would have to feel clumsy and amateurish in the midst of this turmoil of war and duties and rights. How little becomes conscious to us! How often does this little lead to error and confusion! Consciousness is a tool, after all, and considering how much and what great things are accomplished without it one cannot call it the most necessary or the most admirable tool. On the contrary, there is, perhaps, no organ which is so poorly developed, or one that works with so many flaws. It just is the youngest organ, still in its infancy—let's pardon its childish pranks! (To these belong, among many other things, our morality, the sum total of all past value judgments about the actions and attitudes of humanity.)

Therefore we have to reverse the order of ranking: everything "conscious" is only secondary in importance.

That it is closer and more intimate for us is no reason, at least no moral reason, to classify it otherwise. That we consider that which is closest also more important—that is only an old prejudice. Hence: re-learn!—as far as valuing is concerned. Everything mental is to be perceived as the sign language of the body!

Moral Philosophy

In the enormous variety of the activities within an organism the part that becomes conscious is only a means. The little bit of "virtue," "unselfishness," and similar fictions are given the lie in the most radical way by the totality of all the other activities. We are well advised to study our organism in its complete immorality . . .

The animal functions are, after all, immeasurably more important than all beautiful states and heights of consciousness. The latter are surplus, as far as they need not be tools for the animal functions. The entire *conscious* life, the mind and the soul, the heart and goodness, as well as virtue—in whose service does it work? In the service of the highest perfection of the means (means of improving nourishment) of the basic animal functions—most of all of the intensification of life!

There is so much more to what used to be called "body" or "flesh"! The rest consists just of additions. The task of continuing the chain of life, in a way which makes life ever more powerful—that is to be aimed at.

But now look how heart, soul, virtue, and mind almost conspire to this principal task—as if *they* were the ultimate goal! The perversion of life is essentially brought about by the extraordinary capability of error on the part of consciousness. Consciousness is least controlled by instincts, therefore it goes astray most profoundly and for the longest time.

To judge whether existence has value or not by means of the feelings of pleasure and pain — is there any more fantastic excess of vanity? Consciousness is only a means, and feelings of pleasure and pain are also just means!

How is value measured objectively? Only in terms of the quantity of intensified and organized power!

The Will To Power

Charles Baudelaire: "The Giantess"

This poem is a humorous version of over-compensation. While much of the mores of the age tried to play down or deny the importance of the body, favoring visions of the refined soul or the disembodied spirit, this text defiantly glorifies the unsublimated flesh and its animalistic experience — literally enlarging the physical being of the praised woman into gigantic proportions. At the time, such a celebration of the physical was as offensive to the general reading audience as Freud's discovery of infant sexuality was to be later.

When Nature in her potent drives
Conceived some monstrous offspring every day,
I would have liked to live around a young
Giantess, like a voluptuous cat in a queen's lap.

I would have liked to see her body flower with her soul,
Growing freely in its terrifying plays;
Guess if her heart concealed a somber flame
Of humid fogs which might swim in her eyes;

Peruse with leisure her stupendous forms,
Climb on the cliffs of her enormous knees;
And in the summer, under burning suns, when

She is stretching out across the plains.
Sleep in the shadow of her breasts, at ease
— a peaceful village at a mountain's base.

Walt Whitman: "I Sing The Body Electric"

Whitman (1819-1892) was another nineteenth century intellectual who rebelled against the often hypocritical spiritualism of the mainstream culture. "I Sing The Body Electric" (published 1855 in the first edition of Leaves of Grass*) is an unabashed celebration of the corporeal side of human nature—a feat which helped to give his work the bad reputation which it had among the majority of his contemporaries. Whitman was at least half a century ahead of his time—in what he said, and in the way he said it. During most of his life he published and re-published* Leaves of Grass *at his own expense, and he never sold many copies. He had trouble with the courts because of the book's alleged obscenity, and he lost a job in Washington because of his work's reputation. Only a few of his contemporaries recognized Whitman's genius, among them Emerson, who wrote to him: "I greet you at the beginning of a great career." (But even Emerson felt very embarrassed when Whitman published his letter of praise.) In the 1870's, Whitman was discovered by European literati, and only then did his fame slowly take hold in his native land.*

The following excerpts are parts 1, 2, and 9 of "I Sing The Body Electric."

I sing the body electric;
The armies of those I love engirth me, and I engirth them,
They will not let me off till I go with them, respond to them,
And discorrupt them, and charge them full with the charge of
    the soul.

Was it doubted that those who corrupt their own bodies
 conceal themselves?
And if those who defile the living are as bad as they who defile
 the dead?
And if the body does not do fully as much as the soul?
And if the body were not the soul, what is the soul?

*

The love of the body of man or woman balks account, the body
 itself balks account,
That of the male is perfect, and that of the female is perfect.

The expression of the face balks account,
But the expression of a well-made man appears not only in his
 face,
It is in his limbs and joints also, it is curiously in the joints of
 his hips and wrists,
It is in his walk, the carriage of his neck, the flex of his waist
 and knees, dress does not hide him,
The strong sweet quality he has strikes through the cotton and
 broadcloth,
To see him pass conveys as much as the best poem, perhaps
 more,
You linger to see his back, and the back of his neck and
 Shoulder-side.

The sprawl and fulness of babes, the bosoms and heads of
 women, the folds of their dress, their style as we pass in
 the street, the contour of their shape downwards,
The swimmer naked in the swimming-bath, seen as he swims
 through the transparent green-shine, or lies with his face
 up and rolls silently to and fro in the heave of the water,
The bending forward and backward of rowers in row-boats, the
 horseman in his saddle,
Girls, mothers, house-keepers, in all their performances,
The group of laborers seated at noon-time with their open
 dinner-kettles, and their wives waiting,
The female soothing a child, the farmer's daughter in the
 garden or cow-yard,

The young fellow hoeing corn, the sleigh-driver driving his six horses through the crowd,
The wrestle of wrestlers, two apprentice-boys, quite grown, lusty, good natured, native-born, out on the vacant lot at sundown after work,
The coats and caps thrown down, the embrace of love and resistance,
The upper-hold and under-hold, the hair rumpled over and blinding the eyes:
The march of firemen in their own costumes, the play of masculine muscle through clean-setting trowsers and waist-straps,
The slow return from the fire, the pause when the bell strikes suddenly again, and the listening on the alert,
The natural, perfect, varied attitudes, the bent head, the curv'd neck and the counting;
Such-like I love — I loosen myself, pass freely, am at the mother's breast with the little child,
Swim with the swimmers, wrestle with wrestlers, march in line with the firemen, and pause, listen, count.

*

O my body! I dare not desert the likes of you in other men and women, nor the likes of the parts of you,
I believe the likes of you are to stand or fall with the likes of the soul, (and that they are the soul)
I believe the likes of you shall stand or fall with my poems, and that they are my poems,
Man's, woman's, child's, youth's, wife's, husband's, mother's, father's, young man's, young woman's poems,
Head, neck, hair, ears, drop and tympan of the ears,
Eyes, eye-fringes, iris of the eye, eyebrows, and the waking or sleeping of the lids,
Mouth, tongue, lips, teeth, roof of the mouth, jaws, and the jaw-hinges,
Nose, nostrils of the nose, and the partition,
Cheeks, temples, forehead, chin, throat, back of the neck, neck-slue,
Strong shoulders, manly beard, scapula, hind-shoulders, and the ample side-round of the chest,

Upper-arm, armpit, elbow-socket, lower-arm, arm-sinews, arm-bones,
Wrist and wrist-joints, hand, palm, knuckles, thumb, forefinger, finger-joints, finger nails,
Broad breast-front, curling hair of the breast, breast-bone, breast-side,
Ribs, belly, backbone, joints of the backbone,
Hips, hip-sockets, hip-strength, inward and outward round, man-balls, man-root,
Strong set of thighs, well carrying the trunk above,
Leg-fibres, knee, knee-pan, upper-leg, under-leg,
Ankles, instep, foot-ball, toes, toe-joints, the heel;
All attitudes, all the shapeliness, all the belongings of my or your body or of anyone's body, male or female,
The lung-sponges, the stomach-sac, the bowels sweet and clean,
The brain in its folds inside the skull-frame,
Sympathies, heart-valves, palate-valves, sexuality, maternity,
Womanhood, and all that is a woman, and the man that comes from woman,
The womb, the teats, nipples, breast-milk, tears, laughter, weeping, love-looks, love-perturbations and risings,
The voice, articulation, language, whispering, shouting aloud,
Food, drink, pulse, digestion, sweat, sleep, walking, swimming,
Poise on the hips, leaping, reclining, embracing, arm-curving and tightening,
The continual changes of the flex of the mouth, and around the eyes,
The skin, the sunburnt shade, freckles, hair,
The curious sympathy one feels when feeling with the hand the naked meat of the body,
The circling rivers the breath, and breathing it in and out,
The beauty of the waist, and thence of the hips, and thence downward toward the knees,
The thin red jellies within you or within me, the bones and the marrow in the bones,
The exquisite realization of health;
O I say these are not the parts and poems of the body only, but of the soul,
O I say now these are the soul!

XI. THE SELF AS AWARENESS

Self Determination

Henry D. Thoreau: *Walden*

AUTHOR AND TEXT: *Henry David Thoreau (1817-1862), later acclaimed as one of America's greatest literary figures, was an unsuccessful writer and social oddball. He graduated from Harvard, but preferred to work most of his life as a handyman and occasional surveyor. A few times he lived as a caretaker in the house of his friend Emerson. His ideal was to waste as little time as possible on making a living, and to spend as much time as possible on reading, writing, exploring himself, and contemplating nature. In 1854 he published* Walden, *his major work, from which the following selections are taken.*

Thoreau was opposed to the war of the United States against Mexico (in which the U.S. annexed almost half of the Mexican territory). As a sign of protest Thoreau refused to pay his taxes, which earned him a jail sentence. (He was bailed out after one night by an unknown benefactor.) In connection with this incident he wrote "The Duty to Civil Disobedience," an essay which had a significant influence in the twentieth century as a document advocating non-violent resistance against unjust claims of the state. Gandhi, e.g., was strongly influenced by it in his struggle against the British occupation of India. Few people know that Thoreau also wrote two defenses of the violent actions of John Brown, "A Plea for Captain John Brown" (1859), and "The Last Days of John Brown" (1860). Since so much hypocrisy is displayed in connection with the issue of Thoreau and non-violence, a short quotation from his "Plea" is in order: "The slave-ship is on her way, crowded with dying victims; new cargoes are being added in mid-ocean; a small crew of slaveholders, countenanced by a large body of passengers, is smothering four millions under the hatches, and yet the politicians assert that the only proper way by which deliverance is to be obtained is by 'the quiet diffusion of the sentiment of humanity' without any 'outbreak.' As if the sentiments of humanity were ever found unaccompanied by its deeds,..."

THE SELF AS AWARENESS   171

INNER CHANGE VERSUS EXTERNAL CHANGE: *Thoreau is often claimed as a patron of those who oppose social revolutions, while advocating a revolution of minds and individual lives. And social revolutionaries often denounce him as a quietist, a "bourgeois individualist," or as something of the sort. Upon reading Thoreau's many analyses of everyday life carefully it is hard to imagine how anything can change for the better unless both kinds of revolution are involved. To oppose a war mentally while condoning it by going about one's business as usual (let alone supporting it by paying taxes) is certainly a questionable attitude. But rallying en masse against a war while at the same time being incapable of conducting even committee meetings without bloated egos, rivalries, and hidden hostilities is equally suspicious. No social revolution will amount to much if people continue getting their satisfaction from climbing in social hierarchies, collecting medals, or consuming more material goods than they need. But no inner change will amount to too much either if through pollution, bad social relations, and, finally, wars, the earth is made so unlivable that the inner life becomes a desperate retreat. To keep water drinkable, to educate the children in a humane way, or to prevent the stockpiling of ever more warheads and poisonous gas—these are clearly things which cannot be done by disregarding either inner attitudes or social actions.*

~ ~ ~

I would fain say something, not so much concerning the Chinese and Sandwich Islanders as you who read these pages, who are said to live in New England; something about your condition, especially your outward condition or circumstances in this world, in this town, what it is, whether it is necessary that it be as bad as it is, whether it cannot be improved as well as not. I have travelled a good deal in Concord; and, everywhere, in shops, and in offices and fields, the inhabitants have appeared to me to be doing penance in a thousand remarkable ways. What I have heard of Brahmins sitting exposed to four fires and looking in the face of the sun; or hanging suspended, with their heads downwards, over flames; or looking at the heavens over their shoulders "until it becomes impossible for them to resume their natural position, while from the twist of the neck nothing but liquids can pass into the stomach"; or dwelling, chained for life, at the foot of a tree; or measuring with their bodies, like caterpillars, the breadth of vast empires; or standing on one leg on the tops of pillars, — even these forms of conscious penance are hardly more incredible and astonishing than the scenes which I daily witness. The twelve labors of Hercules were trifling in comparison with those which my neighbors have undertaken; for they were only twelve, and had an end; but I could never see that these men slew or captured any monster or finished any labor. They have no friend Iolaus to burn with a hot iron the root of the hydra's head, but as soon as one head is crushed, two spring up.

*

Most men, even in this comparatively free country, through mere ignorance and mistake, are so occupied with the factitious cares and superfluously coarse labor of life that its finer fruits cannot be plucked by them. Their fingers, from excessive toil, are too clumsy and tremble too much for that. Actually, the laboring man has not leisure for a true integrity day by day; he cannot afford to sustain the manliest relations to men; his labor would be depreciated in the market. He has no time to be anything but a machine. How can he remember well his ignorance — which his growth requires — who has so often to use his knowledge? We should feed and clothe him gratuitously sometimes, and recruit him with our cordials, before we judge of him. The finest qualities of our nature, like the bloom on fruits, can be preserved only by the most delicate handling. Yet we do not treat ourselves nor one another thus tenderly.

*

I sometimes wonder that we can be so frivolous, I may almost say, as to attend to the gross but somewhat foreign form of servitude called Negro Slavery, there are so many keen and subtle masters that enslave both North and South. It is hard to have a Southern overseer; it is worse to have a Northern one; but the worst of all when you are the slave-driver of yourself. Talk of a divinity in man! Look at the teamster on the highway, wending to market by day or night; does any divinity stir within him? His highest duty to fodder and water his horses! What is his destiny to him compared with the shipping interests? Does not he drive for Squire Make-a-stir? How godlike, how immortal, is he? See how he cowers and sneaks, how vaguely all the day he fears, not being immortal nor divine, but the slave and prisoner of his own opinion of himself, a fame won by his own deeds. Public opinion is a weak tyrant compared with our own private opinion. What a man thinks of himself, that it is which determines, or rather indicates, his fate. Self-emancipation even in the West Indian provinces of the fancy and imagination, — what Wilberforce is there to bring that about? Think, also, of the ladies of the land weaving toilet cushions against the last day, not to betray too green an interest in their fates! As if you could kill time without injuring eternity.

The mass of men lead lives of quiet desperation. What is called resignation is confirmed desperation. From the desperate city you go into the desperate country, and have to console yourself with the bravery of minks and muskrats. A stereotyped but unconscious despair is concealed even under what are called the games and amusements of mankind. There is no play in them, for this comes after work. But it is a characteristic of wisdom not to do desperate things.

*

Most of the luxuries, and many of the so-called comforts of life, are not only not indispensable, but positive hindrances to the elevation of mankind. With respect to luxuries and comforts, the wisest have ever lived a more simple and meagre life than the poor. The ancient philosophers, Chinese, Hindoo, Persian, and Greek, were a class than which none has been poorer in outward riches, none so rich in inward. We know not much about them. It is remarkable that *we* know so much of them as we do. The same is true of the more modern reformers and benefactors of their race. None can be an impartial or wise observer of human life but from the vantage ground of what *we* should call voluntary poverty. Of a life of luxury the fruit is luxury, whether in agriculture, or commerce, or literature, or art. There are nowadays professors of philosophy, but not philosophers. Yet it is admirable to profess because it was once admirable to live. To be a philosopher is not merely to have subtle thoughts, nor even to found a school, but so to love wisdom as to live according to its dictates, a life of simplicity, independence, magnanimity, and trust. It is to solve some of the problems of life, not only theoretically, but practically. The success of great scholars and thinkers is commonly a courtier-like success, not kingly, not manly. They make shift to live merely by conformity, practically as their fathers did, and are in no sense the progenitors of a nobler race of men. But why do men degenerate ever? What makes families run out? What is the nature of the luxury which enervates and destroys nations? Are we sure that there is none of it in our own lives? The philosopher is in advance of his age even in the outward form of his life. He is not fed, sheltered, clothed, warmed, like his contemporaries. How can a man be a philosopher and not maintain his vital heat by better methods than other men?

When a man is warmed by the several modes which I have described, what does he want next? Surely not more warmth of the same kind, as more and richer food, larger and more splendid houses, finer and more abundant clothing, more numerous, incessant, and hotter fires, and the like. When he has obtained those things which are necessary to life, there is another alternative than to obtain the superfluities; and that is, to adventure on life now, his vacation from humbler toil having commenced. The soil, it appears, is suited to the seed, for it has sent its radicle downward, and it may now send its shoot upward also with confidence. Why has man rooted himself thus firmly in the earth, but that he may rise in the same proportion into the heavens above? — for the nobler plants are valued for the fruit they bear at last in the air and light, far from the ground, and are not treated like the humbler esculents, which, though they may be biennial, are cut down at top for this purpose, so that most would not know them in their flowering season.

*

As this business was to be entered into without the usual capital, it may not be easy to conjecture where those means, that will still be indispensable to every such undertaking, were to be obtained. As for clothing, to come at once to the practical part of the question, perhaps we are led oftener by the love of novelty and a regard for the opinions of men, in procuring it, than by a true utility. Let him that has work to do recollect that the object of clothing is, first, to retain the vital heat, and secondly, in this state of society, to cover nakedness, and he may judge how much of any necessary or important work may be accomplished without adding to his wardrobe. Kings and queens who wear a suit but once, though made by some tailor or dressmaker to their majesties, cannot know the comfort of wearing a suit that fits. They are no better than wooden horses to hang the clean clothes on. Every day our garments become more assimilated to ourselves, receiving the impress of the wearer's character, until we hesitate to lay them aside without such delay and medical appliances and some such solemnity even as our bodies. No man ever stood the lower in my estimation for having a patch in his clothes; yet I am sure that there is greater anxiety, commonly, to have fashionable, or at least clean and unpatched clothes, than to have a sound conscience. But even if the rent is not mended, perhaps the worst vice betrayed is improvidence. I sometimes try my acquaintances by such tests as this,—Who could wear a patch, or two extra seams only, over the knee? Most behave as if they believed that their prospects for life would be ruined if they should do it. It would be easier for them to hobble to town with a broken leg than with a broken pantaloon. Often if an accident happens to a gentlemen's legs, they can be mended; but if a similar accident happens to the legs of his pantaloons, there is no help for it; for he considers, not what is truly respectable, but what is respected. We know but few men, a great many coats and breeches. Dress a scarecrow in your last shift, you standing shiftless by, who would not soonest salute the scarecrow? Passing a cornfield the other day, close by a hat and coat on a stake, I recognized the owner of the farm. He was only a little more weatherbeaten than when I saw him last. I have heard of a dog that barked at every stranger who approached his master's premises with clothes on, but was easily quieted by a naked thief. It is an interesting question how far men would retain their relative rank if they were divested of their clothes. Could you, in such a case, tell surely of any company of civilized men which belonged to the most respected class? Madam Pfeiffer, in her adventurous travels round the world, from east to west, had got so near home as Asiatic Russia, she says that she felt the necessity of wearing other than a traveling dress, when she went to meet the authorities, for she "was now in a civilized country, where . . . people are judged of by their clothes." Even in our democratic New England towns the accidental possession of wealth, and its manifestation in dress and equipage alone, obtain for the possessor almost universal respect. But they who yield such respect, numerous as they are. are so far heathen, and need to have a missionary sent to them. Beside, clothes introduced sewing. a kind of work which you may call endless; a woman's dress, at least, is never done.

A man who has at length found something to do will not need to get a new suit to do it in; for him the old will do, that has lain dusty in the garret for an indeterminate period. Old shoes will serve a hero longer than they have served his valet—if a hero ever has a valet,—bare feet are older than shoes, and he can make them do. Only they who go to soirees and legislative halls must have new coats, coats to change as often as the man changes in them. But if my jacket and trousers, my hat and shoes, are fit to worship God in, they will do; will they not? Who ever saw his old clothes,—his old coat, actually worn out, resolved into its primitive elements, so that it was not a deed of charity to bestow it on some poor boy, by him perchance to be bestowed on some poorer still, or shall we say richer, who could do with less? I say. beware of all enterprises that require new clothes, and not rather a new wearer of clothes. If there is not a new man. how can the new clothes be made to fit? If you have any enterprise before you, try it in your old clothes. All men want, not something to *do with*, but something to *do*, or rather something to *be*. Perhaps we should never procure a new suit. however ragged or dirty the old, until we have so conducted, so enterprised or sailed in some way, that we feel like new men in the old, and that to retain it would be like keeping new wine in old bottles. Our molting season, like that of the fowls, must be a crisis in our lives. The loon retires to solitary ponds to spend it. Thus also the snake casts its slough, and the caterpillar its wormy coat, by an internal industry and expansion; for clothes are but our outmost cuticle and moral coil. Otherwise we shall be found sailing under false colors, and be inevitably cashiered at last by our own opinion, as well as that of mankind.

We don garment after garment, as if we grew like exogenous plants by addition without. Our outside and often thin and fanciful clothes are our epidermis, or false skin, which partakes not of our life, and may be stripped off here and there without fatal injury; our thicker garments, constantly worn, are our cellular integument, or cortex; but our shirts are our liber, or true bark, which cannot be removed without girdling and so destroying the man. I believe that all races at some seasons wear something equivalent to the shirt. It is desirable that a man be clad so simply that he can lay his hands on himself in the dark, and that he live in all respects so compactly and preparedly that, if an enemy take the town, he can, like the old philosopher, walk out the gate empty-handed without anxiety. While one thick garment is, for most purposes, as good as three thin ones, and cheap clothing can be obtained at prices really to suit customers; while a thick coat can be bought for five dollars, which will last as many years, thick pantaloons for two dollars, cowhide boots for a dollar and a half a pair, a summer hat for a quarter of a dollar, and a winter cap for sixty-two and a half cents, or a better be made at home at a nominal cost, where is he so poor that, clad in such a suit, *of his own earning*, there will not be found wise men to do him reverence?

When I ask for a garment of a particular form, my tailoress tells me gravely, "They do not make them so now," not emphasizing the "They" at all, as if she quoted an authority as impersonal as the Fates, and I find it difficult to get made what I want, simply because she cannot believe that I mean what I say, that I am so rash. When I hear this oracular sentence, I am for a moment absorbed in thought, emphasizing to myself each word separately that I may come at the meaning of it, that I may find out by what degree of consanguinity *they* are related to *me*, and what authority they may have in an affair which affects me so nearly; and, finally, I am inclined to answer her with equal mystery, and without any more emphasis of the "They,"—"It is true, they did not make them so recently, but they do now." Of what use this measuring of me if she does not measure my character, but only the breadth of my shoulders, as it were a peg to hang to coat on? We worship not the Graces, nor the Parcae, but Fashion. She spins and weaves and cuts with full authority. The head monkey at Paris puts on a traveller's cap, and all the monkeys in America do the same. I sometimes despair of getting anything quite simple and honest done in this world by the help of men. They would have to be passed through a powerful press first, to squeeze their old notions out of them, so that they would not soon get upon their legs again; and then there would be some one in the company with a maggot in his head, hatched from an egg deposited there nobody knows when, for not even fire kills these things, and you would have lost your labor. Nevertheless, we will not forget that some Egyptian wheat was handed down to us by a mummy.

On the whole, I think it cannot be maintained that dressing has in this or any country risen to the dignity of an art. At present men make shift to wear what they can get. Like shipwrecked sailors, they put on what they can find on the beach, and at a little distance, whether of space or time, laugh at each other's masquerade. Every generation laughs at the old fashions, but follows religiously the new. We are amused at beholding the costume of Henry VII, or Queen Elizabeth, as much as if it was that of the King and Queen of the Cannibal Islands. All costume off a man is pitiful or grotesque. It is only the serious eye peering from and the life passed within it which restrain laughter and consecrate the costume of any people. Let Harlequin be taken with a fit of colic and his trappings will have to serve that mood too. When the soldier is hit by a cannonball, rags are as becoming as purple.

The childish and savage taste of men and women for new patterns keeps how many shaking and squinting through kaleidoscopes that they may discover the particular figure which this generation requires to-day. The manufacturers have learned that this taste is merely whimsical. Of two patterns which differ only by a few threads more or less of a particular color, the one will be sold readily, the other lie on the shelf, though it frequently happens that after the lapse of a season the latter becomes the most fashionable. Comparatively, tattooing is not the hideous custom which it is called. It is not barbarous merely because the printing is skin-deep and unalterable.

I cannot believe that our factory system is the best mode by which men may get clothing. The condition of the operatives is becoming every day more like that of the English; and it cannot be wondered at, since, as far as I have heard or observed, the principal object is, not that mankind may be well and honestly clad, but, unquestionably, that the corporations may be enriched. In the long run men hit only what they aim at. Therefore, though they should fail immediately, they had better aim at something high.

*

In the savage state every family owns a shelter as good as the best, and sufficient for its coarser and simpler wants; but I think that I speak within the bounds when I say that, though the birds of the air have their nests, and the foxes their holes, and the savages their wigwams, in modern civilized society not more than one half the families own a shelter. In the large towns and cities, where civilization especially prevails, the number of those who own a shelter is a very small fraction of the whole. The rest pay an annual tax for this outside garment of all, become indispensable summer and winter, which would buy a village of Indian wigwams, but now helps to keep them poor as long as they live. I do not mean to insist here on the disadvantage of hiring compared with owning, but it is evident that the savage owns his shelter because it costs so little, while the civilized man hires his commonly because he cannot afford to own it; nor can he, in the long run, any better afford to hire.

But, answers one, by merely paying this tax the poor civilized man secures an abode which is a palace compared with the savage's. An annual rent of from twenty-five to a hundred dollars (these are the country rates) entitles him to the benefit of the improvements of centuries, spacious apartments, clean paint and paper, Rumford fireplace, back plastering, Venetian blinds, copper pump, spring lock, a commodious cellar, and many other things. But how happens it that he who is said to enjoy these things is so commonly a *poor* civilized man, while the savage, who has them not, is rich as a savage? If it is asserted that civilization is a real advance in the condition of man,—and I think that it is, though only the wise improve their advantages,—it must be shown that it has produced better dwellings without making them more costly; and the cost of a thing is the amount of what I will call life which is required to be exchanged for it, immediately or in the long run. An average house in this neighborhood costs perhaps eight hundred dollars, and to lay up this sum will take from ten to fifteen years of the laborer's life, even if he is not encumbered with a family,—estimating the pecuniary value of every man's labor at one dollar a day, for if some receive more, others receive less;—so that he must have spent more than half his life commonly before his wigwam will be earned. If we suppose him to pay a rent instead, this is but a doubtful choice of evils. Would a savage have been wise to exchange his wigwam for a palace on these terms?

*

Granted that the *majority* are able at last either to own or hire the modern house with all its improvements. While civilization has been improving our houses, it has not equally improved the men who are to inhabit them. It has created palaces, but it was not so easy to create noblemen and kings. And *if the civilized man's pursuits are not worthier than the savage's, if he is employed the greater part of his life in obtaining gross necessaries and comforts merely, why should he have a better dwelling than the former?*

But how do the poor *minority* fare? Perhaps it will be found that just in proportion as some have been placed in outward circumstances above the savage, others have been degraded below him. The luxury of one class is counterbalanced by the indigence of another. On the one side is the palace, on the other are the almshouse and "silent poor." The myriads who built the pyramids to be the tombs of the Pharaohs were fed on garlic, and it may be were not decently buried themselves. The mason who finishes the cornice of the palace returns at night perchance to a hut not so good as a wigwam. It is a mistake to suppose that, in a country where the usual evidences of civilization exist, the condition of a very large body of the inhabitants may not be as degraded as that of savages. I refer to the degraded poor, not now to the degraded rich. To know this I should not need to look farther than to the shanties which everywhere border our railroads, that last improvement in civilization; where I see in my daily walks human beings living in sties, and all winter with an open door, for the sake of light, without any visible, often imaginable, wood-pile, and the forms of both old and young are permanently contracted by the long habit of shrinking from cold and misery, and the development of all their limbs and faculties is checked. It certainly is fair to look at that class by whose labor the works which distinguish this generation are accomplished. Such too, to a greater or less extent, is the condition of the operatives of every denomination in England, which is the great workhouse of the world. Or I could refer you to Ireland, which is marked as one of the white or enlightened spots on the map. Contrast the physical condition of the Irish with that of the North American Indian, or the South Sea Islander, or any other savage race before it was degraded by contact with the civilized man. Yet I have no doubt that that peoples' rulers are as wise as the average of civilized rulers. Their condition only proves what squalidness may consist with civilization. I hardly need refer now to the laborers in our Southern States who produce the staple exports of this country, and are themselves a staple production of the South. But to confine my self to those who are said to be in *moderate* circumstances.

Most men appear never to have considered what a house is, and are actually though needlessly poor all their lives because they think that they must have such a one as their neighbors have. As if one were to wear any sort of coat which the tailor might cut out for him, or, gradually leaving off palm-leaf hat or cap of woodchuck skin, complain of hard times because he could not afford to buy him a crown! It is possible to invent a house still more convenient and luxurious than we have, which yet all would admit that man could not afford to pay for. Shall we always study to obtain most of these things, and not sometimes to be content with less? Shall the respectable citizen thus gravely teach, by precept and example, the necessity of the young man's providing a certain number of superfluous glow-shoes, and umbrellas, and empty guest chambers for empty guests, before he dies? Why should not our furniture be as simple as the Arab's or the Indian's? When I think of the benefactors of the race, whom we have apotheosized as messengers from heaven, bearers of divine gifts to man, I do not see in my mind any retinue at their heels, any carloads of fashionable furniture. Or what if I were to allow—would it not be a singular allowance?—that our furniture should be more complex than the Arab's, in proportion as we are morally and intellectually his superiors! At present our houses are cluttered and defiled with it, and a good housewife would sweep out the greater part into the dust hole, and not leave her morning's work undone. Morning work! By the blushes of Aurora and the music of Memnon, what should be man's *morning* work in this world? I had three pieces of limestone on my desk, but I was terrified to find that they required to be dusted daily, when the furniture of my mind was all undusted still, and I threw them out the window in disgust. How, then, could I have a furnished house? I would rather sit in the open air, for no dust gathers on the grass, unless where man has broken ground.

It is the luxurious and dissipated who set the fashions which the herd so diligently follow. The traveller who stops at the best houses, so called, soon discovers this, for the publicans presume him to be a Sardanapalus, and if he resigned himself to their tender mercies he would soon be completely emasculated. I think that in the railroad car we are inclined to spend more on luxury than on safety and convenience, and it threatens without attaining these to become no better than a modern drawing room, with its divans and ottomans, and sun-shades, and a hundred other oriental things, which we are taking west with us, invented for the ladies of the harem and the effeminate natives of the Celestial Empire, which Jonathan should be ashamed to know the names of. I would rather sit on a pumpkin and have it all to myself than be crowded on a velvet cushion. I would rather ride on earth in an ox cart, with a free circulation, than go to heaven in the fancy car of an excursion train and breathe a *malaria* all the way.

The very simplicity and nakedness of man's life in the primitive ages imply this advantage, at least, that they left him still but a sojourner in nature. When he was refreshed with food and sleep, he contemplated his journey again. He dwelt, as it were, in a tent in this world, and was either threading the valleys, or crossing the plains, or climbing the mountaintops. But lo! men have become the tools of their tools. The man who independently plucked the fruits when he was hungry is become a farmer; and he who stood under a tree for shelter, a housekeeper. We now no longer camp as for a night, but have settled down on earth and forgotten heaven. We have adopted Christianity merely as an improved method of *agri*-culture. We have built for this world a family mansion, and for the next a family tomb. The best works of art are the expression of man's struggle to free himself from this condition, but the effect of our art is merely to make this low state comfortable and that higher state to be forgotten. There is actually no place in this village for a work of fine art, if any had come down to us, to stand, for our lives, our houses and streets, furnish no proper pedestal for it. There is not a nail to hang a picture on, nor a shelf to receive the bust of a hero or a saint. When I consider how our houses are built and paid for, or not paid for, and their internal economy managed and sustained, I wonder that the floor does not give way under the visitor while he is admiring the gewgaws upon the mantelpiece, and let him through into the cellar to some solid and honest though earthly foundation. I cannot but perceive that this so-called rich and refined life is a thing jumped at, and I do not get on in the enjoyment of the *fine* arts which adorn it, my attention being wholly occupied with the jump; for I remember that the greatest genuine leap, due to human muscles alone, on record, is that of certain wandering Arabs, who are said to have cleared twenty-five feet on level ground. Without factitious support, man is sure to come to earth again beyond that distance. The first question which I am tempted to put to the proprietor of such great impropriety is, Who bolsters you? Are you one of the ninety-seven who fail, or the three who succeed? Answer me these questions, and then perhaps I may look at your baubles and find them ornamental. The cart before the horse is neither beautiful nor useful. Before we can adorn our houses with beautiful objects the walls must be stripped, and our lives must be stripped, and beautiful housekeeping and beautiful living be laid for a foundation: now, a taste for the beautiful is most cultivated out of doors, where there is no house and no housekeeper.

*

It would be worth the while to build still more deliberately than I did, considering, for instance, what foundation a door, a window, a cellar, a garret, have in the nature of man, and perchance never raising any superstructure until we found a better reason for it than our temporal necessities even. There is some of the same fitness in a man's building his own house than there is in a bird's building its own nest. Who knows but if men constructed their dwellings with their own hands, and provided food for themselves and families simply and honestly enough, the poetic faculty would be universally developed, as birds universally sing when they are so engaged! But alas! we do like cowbirds and cuckoos, which lay their eggs in nests which other birds have built, and cheer no traveller with their chattering and unmusical notes. Shall we forever resign the pleasure of construction to the carpenter? What does architecture amount to in the experience of the mass of men? I never in all my walks came across a man engaged in so simple and natural an occupation as building his house. We belong to a community. It is not the tailor alone who is the ninth part of a man; it is as much the preacher, and the merchant, and the farmer. Where is this division of labor to end? and what object does it finally serve? No doubt another *may* also think for me; but it is not therefore desirable that he should do so to the exclusion of my thinking for myself.

True, there are architects so called in this country, and I have heard of one at least possessed with the idea of making architectural ornaments have a core of truth, a necessity, and hence a beauty, as if it were a revelation to him. All very well perhaps from his point of view, but only a little better than the common dilettantism. A sentimental reformer in architecture, he began at the cornice, not at the foundation. It was only how to put a core of truth within the ornaments, that every sugar-plum, in fact, might have an almond or caraway seed in it, — though I hold that almonds are most wholesome without the sugar, — and not how the inhabitant, the indweller, might build truly within and without, and let the ornaments take care of themselves. What reasonable man ever supposed that ornaments were something outward and in the skin merely, — that the tortoise got his spotted shell, or the shellfish its mother-o'-pearl tints, by such a contract as the inhabitants of Broadway their Trinity Church? But a man has no more to do with the style of architecture of his houses than a tortoise with that of its shell: nor need the soldier be so idle as to try to paint the precise *color* of his virtue on his standard. The enemy will find it out. He may turn pale when the trial comes. This man seemed to me to lean over the cornice, and timidly whisper his half truth to the rude occupants who really knew it better than he. What of architectural beauty I now see, I know has gradually grown from within outward, out of the necessities and character of the indweller, who is the only builder, — out of some unconscious truthfulness, and nobleness, without ever a thought for the appearance, and whatever additional beauty of this kind is destined to be produced will be preceded by a like unconscious beauty of life. The most interesting dwellings in this country, as the painter knows, are the most unpretending, humble log huts and cottages of the poor commonly; it is the life of the inhabitants whose shells they are, and not any peculiarity in their surfaces merely, which makes them *picturesque*; and equally interesting will be the citizen's suburban box, when his life shall be as simple and as agreeable to the imagination, and there is as little straining after effect in the style of his dwelling. A great proportion of architectural ornaments are literally hollow, and a September gale would strip them off, like borrowed plumes, without injury to the substantials.

They can do without *architecture* who have no olives nor wines in the cellar. What if an equal ado were made about the ornaments of style in literature, and the architects of our bibles spent as much time about their cornices as the architects of our churches do? So are made the belles-lettres and the beaux-arts and their professors. Much it concerns a man, forsooth, how a few sticks are slanted over him or under him, and what colors are daubed upon his box. It would signify somewhat, if, in any earnest sense, he slanted them and daubed it; but the spirit having departed out of the tenant, it is of a piece with constructing his own coffin; — the architecture of the grave, — and "carpenter" is but another name for "coffin-maker".

*

I thus found that the student who wishes for a shelter can obtain one for a lifetime at an expense not greater than the rent which he now pays annually. If I seem to boast more than is becoming my excuse is that I brag for humanity rather than for myself; and my shortcomings and inconsistencies do not affect the truth of my statement. Notwithstanding much cant and hypocrisy, — chaff which I find it difficult to separate from my wheat, but for which I am as sorry as any man, — I will breathe freely and stretch myself in this respect, it is such a relief to both the moral and physical system; and I am resolved that I will not through humility become the devil's attorney. I will endeavor to speak a good word for the truth. At Cambridge College the mere rent of a student's room, which is only a little larger than my own, is thirty dollars each year, though the corporation had the advantage of building thirty-two side by side and under one roof, and the occupant suffers the inconvenience of many and noisy neighbors, and perhaps a residence in the fourth story. I cannot but think that if we had more true wisdom in these respects, not only less education would be needed, because, forsooth, more would already have been acquired, but the pecuniary expense of getting an education would in a great measure vanish. Those conveniences which the student requires at Cambridge or elsewhere cost him or somebody else ten times as great a sacrifice of life as they would with proper management on both sides. Those things for which the most money is demanded are never the things which the student most wants. Tuition, for instance, is an important item in the term bill, while for the far more valuable education which he gets by associating with the most cultivated of his contemporaries no charge is made. The mode of founding a college is, commonly, to get up a subscription of dollars and cents, and then, following blindly the principles of a division of labor to its extreme, — a principle which should never be followed but with circumspection, — to call in a contractor who makes this a subject of speculation, and he employs Irishmen or other operatives actually to lay the foundations, while the students that are to be are said to be fitting themselves for it; and for these oversights successive generations have to pay. I think that it would be *better than this*, for the students, or those who desire to be benefited by it, even to lay the foundation themselves. The student who secures his coveted leisure and retirement by systematically shirking any labor necessary to man obtains but an ignoble and unprofitable leisure, defrauding himself of the experience which alone can make leisure fruitful. "But," says one, "you do not mean that the students should go to work with their hands instead of their heads?" I do not mean that exactly, but I mean something which he might think a good deal like that; I mean that they should not *play* life, or *study* it merely, while the community supports them at this expensive game, but earnestly *live* it from beginning to end. How could youths better learn to live than by at once trying the experiment of living? Methinks this would exercise their minds as much as mathematics. If I wished a boy to know something about the arts and sciences, for instance, I should not pursue the common course, which is merely to send him into the neighborhood of some professor, where anything is professed and practiced but the art of life; — to survey the world through a telescope or a microscope, and never with his natural eye; to study chemistry, and not learn how his bread is made, or mechanics, and not learn how it is earned; to discover new satellites to Neptune, and not detect the motes in his eyes, or to what vagabond he is a satellite himself; or to be devoured by the monsters that swarm all around him, while contemplating the monsters in a drop of vinegar. Which would have advanced the most at the end of a month, — the boy who had made his own jackknife from the ore which he had dug and smelted, reading as much as would be necessary for this — or the boy who had attended the lectures on metallurgy at the Institute in the meanwhile, and had received a Rodgers penknife from his father? Which would be most likely to cut his fingers? . . . To my astonishment I was informed on leaving college that I had studied navigation! — why, if I had taken one turn down the harbor I should have known more about it. Even the *poor* student studies and is taught only *political* economy, while that economy of living which is synonymous with philosophy is not even sincerely professed in our college. The consequence is, that while he is reading Adam Smith, Ricardo, and Say, he runs his father in debt irretrievably.

As with our colleges, so with a hundred "modern improvements;" there is an illusion about them; there is not always a positive advance. The devil goes on extracting compound interest to the last for his early share and numerous succeeding investments in them. Our inventions are wont to be pretty toys, which distract our attention from serious things. They are but improved means to an unimproved end, an end which it was already but too easy to arrive at; as railroads lead to Boston or New York. We are in great haste to construct a magnetic telegraph form Maine to Texas; but Maine and Texas, it may be, have nothing important to communicate. Either is in such a predicament as the man who was earnest to be introduced to a distinguished deaf woman, but when he was presented, and one end of her ear trumpet was put into his hand, had nothing to say. As if the main object were to talk fast and not to talk sensibly. We are eager to tunnel under the Atlantic and bring the Old World some weeks nearer to the New; but perchance the first news that will leak through into the broad, flapping American ear will be that the Princess Adelaide has the whooping cough. After all, the man whose horse trots a mile in a minute does not carry the most important messages; he is not an evangelist, nor does he come round eating locusts and wild honey. I doubt if Flying Childers ever carried a peck of corn to mill.

*

Such is the universal law, which no man can ever outwit, and with regard to the railroad even we may say it is as broad as it is long. To make a railroad round the world available to all mankind is equivalent to grading the whole surface of the planet. Men have an indistinct notion that if they keep up this activity of joint stocks and spades long enough all will at length ride somewhere, in next to no time, and for nothing; but though a crowd rushes to the depot, and the conductor shouts "All aboard!" when the smoke is blown away and the vapor condensed, it will be perceived that a few are riding, but the rest are run over, — and it will be called, and will be, "A melancholy accident." No doubt they can ride at last who shall have earned their fare, that is, if they survive so long, but they will probably have lost their elasticity and desire to travel by that time. This spending of the best part of one's life earning money in order to enjoy a questionable liberty during the least valuable part of it reminds me of the Englishman who went to India to make a fortune first, in order that he might return to England to live the life of a poet. He should have gone up garret at once. "What!" exclaim a million Irishmen starting up from all the shanties in the land, "is not this railroad which we have built a good thing?" Yes, I answer, *comparatively* good, that is, you might have done worse; but I wish, as you are brothers of mine, that you could have spent your time better than digging in this dirt.

*

I am wont to think that men are not so much the keepers of herds as herds are the keepers of men, the former are so much the freer. Men and oxen exchange work; but if we consider necessary work only, the oxen will be seen to have greatly the advantage, their farm is so much the larger. Man does some of his part of the exchange work in his six weeks of haying, and it is not boy's play. Certainly no nation that lived simply in all respects, that is, no nation of philosophers, would commit so great a blunder as to use the labor of animals. True, there never was and is not likely, soon to be a nation of philosophers, nor am I certain it is desirable that there should be. However, I should never have broken a horse or bull and taken him to board for any work he might do for me, for fear I should become a horse-man or a herds-man merely; and if society seems to be the gainer by so doing, are we certain that what is one man's gain is not another's loss, and that the stableboy has equal cause with his master to be satisfied? Granted that some public works would not have been constructed without this aid, and let man share the glory of such with the ox and horse; does it follow that he could not have accomplished works yet more worthy of himself in that case? When men begin to do, not merely unnecessary or artistic, but luxurious and idle work with their assistance, it is inevitable that a few do all the exchange work with the oxen, or, in other words, become the slaves of the strongest. Man thus not only works for the animal within him, but, for a symbol of this, he works for the animal without him. Though we have many substantial houses of brick or stone, the prosperity of the farmer is still measured by the degree to which the barn overshadows the house. This town is said to have the largest houses for oxen, cows, and horses hereabouts, and it is not behindhand in its public buildings; but there are very few halls for free worship or free speech in this country. It should not be by their architecture, but why not even by their power of abstract thought, that nations should seek to commemorate themselves? How much more admirable the Bhagvat-Geeta than all the ruins of the East! Towers and temples are the luxury of princes. A simple and independent mind does not toil at the bidding of any prince. Genius is not a retainer to any emperor, nor is its material silver, or gold, or marble, except to a trifling extent. To what end, pray, is so much stone hammered? In Arcadia, when I was there, I did not see any hammering stone. Nations are possessed with an insane ambition to perpetuate the memory of themselves by the amount of hammered stone they leave. What if equal pains were taken to smooth and polish their manners? One piece of good sense would be more memorable than a monument as high as the moon. I love better to see stones in place. The grandeur of Thebes was a vulgar grandeur. More sensible is a rod of stone wall that bounds an honest man's field than a hundred-gated Thebes that has wandered farther from the true end of life. The religion and civilization which are barbaric and heathenish build splendid temples; but what you might call Christianity does not. Most of the stone a nation hammers goes toward its tomb only. It buries itself alive. As for the Pyramids, there is nothing to wonder at in them so much as the fact that so many men could be found degraded enough to spend their lives constructing a tomb for some ambitious booby, whom it would have been wiser and manlier to have drowned in the Nile, and then given his body to the dogs. I might possibly invent some excuse for them and him, but I have no time for it. As for the religion and love of art of the builders, it is much the same all the world over, whether the building be an Egyptian temple or the United States Bank. It costs more than it comes to. The mainspring is vanity, assisted by the love of garlic and bread and butter. Mr. Balcom, a promising young architect, designs it on the back of his Vitruvius, with hard pencil and ruler, and the job is let out to Dobson & Sons, stonecutters. When the thirty centuries begin to look down on it, mankind begin to look up at it. As for your high towers and monuments, there was a crazy fellow once in this town who undertook to dig through to China, and he got so far that, as he said, he heard the Chinese pots and kettles rattle; but I think that I shall not go out of my way to admire the hole which he made. Many are concerned about the monuments of the West and the East, — to know who built them. For my part, I should like to know who in those days did not build them, — who were above such trifling.

*

My furniture, part of which I made myself, — and the rest cost me nothing of which I have not rendered an account, — consisted of a bed, a table, a desk, three chairs, a looking glass three inches in diameter, a pair of tongs and andirons, a kettle, a skillet, and a frying-pan, a dipper, a wash-bowl, two knives and forks, three plates, one cup, one spoon, a jug for oil, a jug for molasses, and a japanned lamp. None is so poor that he need sit on a pumpkin. That is shiftlessness. There is a plenty of such chairs as I like best in the village garrets to be had for taking them away. Furniture! Thank God, I can sit and I can stand with the aid of a furniture warehouse. What man but a philosopher would not be ashamed to see his furniture packed in a cart and going up country exposed to the light of heaven and the eyes of men, a beggarly account of empty boxes? That is Spaulding furniture. I could never tell from inspecting such a load whether it belonged to a so-called rich man or a poor one; the owner always seemed poverty-stricken. Indeed, the more you have of such things the poorer you are. Each load looks as if it contained the contents of a dozen shanties; and if one shanty is poor, this is a dozen times as poor. Pray, for what do we move ever but to get rid of our furniture, our *exuviae*; at last to go from this world to another newly furnished, and leave this to be burned? It is the same as if all these traps were buckled to a man's belt, and he could not move over the rough country where our lines are cast without dragging them,—dragging his trap. He was a lucky fox that left his tail in the trap. The muskrat will gnaw his third leg off to be free. No wonder man has lost his elasticity. How often he is at a dead set! "Sir, if I may be so bold, what do you mean by a dead set?" If you are a seer whenever you meet a man you will see all that he owns, ay, and much that he pretends to disown, behind him, even to his kitchen furniture and all the trumpery which he saves and will not burn, and he will appear to be harnessed to it and making what headway he can. I think that the man is at a dead set who has got through a knot-hole or gateway where his sledge load of furniture cannot follow him. I cannot but feel compassion when I hear some trig, compact-looking man, seemingly free, all girded and ready, speak of his "furniture," as whether it is insured or not. "But what shall I do with my furniture?" My gay butterfly is entangled in a spider's web then. Even those who seem for a long while not to have any, if you inquire more narrowly you will find have some stored in somebody's barn. I look upon England to-day as a gentleman who is travelling with a great deal of baggage, trumpery which has accumulated from long housekeeping, which he has not the courage to burn; great trunk, little trunk, bandbox, and bundle. Throw away the first three at least. It would surpass the powers of a well man nowadays to take up his bed and walk, and I should certainly advise a sick one to lay down his bed and run. When I have met an immigrant tottering under a bundle which contained his all,—looking like an enormous wen which had grown out of the nape of his neck, — I have pitied him, not because that was his all, but because he had all *that* to carry. If I have got to drag my trap, I will take care that it be a light one and do not nip me in a vital part. But perchance it would be wisest never to put one's paw into it.

I would observe, by the way, that it costs me nothing for curtains, for I have no gazers to shut out but the sun and moon, and I am willing that they should look in. The moon will not sour milk nor taint meat of mine, nor will the sun injure my furniture or fade my carpet; and if he is sometimes too warm a friend, I find it still better economy to retreat behind some curtain which nature has provided, than to add a single item to the details of housekeeping. A lady once offered me a mat, but as I had no room to spare within the house, nor time to spare within or without to shake it, I declined it, preferring to wipe my feet on the sod before my door. It is best to avoid the beginnings of evil.

Not long since I was present at the auction of a deacon's effects, for his life had not been ineffectual: —

"The evil that men do lives after them."

As usual, a great proportion was trumpery which had begun to accumulate in his father's day. Among the rest was a dried tapeworm. And now, after lying half a century in his garret and other dust holes, these things were not burned; instead of a *bonfire,* or purifying destruction of them, there was an *auction,* or increasing of them. The neighbors eagerly collected to view them, bought them all, and carefully transported them to their garrets and dust holes, to lie there till their estates are settled, when they will start again. When a man dies he kicks the dust.

The customs of some savage nations might, perchance, be profitably imitated by us, for they at least go through the semblance of casting their slough annually; they have the idea of the thing, whether they have the reality or not. Would it not be well if we were to celebrate such a "busk," or "feast of the first fruits," as Bartram describes to have been the custom of the Mucclasse Indians? "When a town celebrates the busk," says he, "having previously provided themselves with new clothes, new pots, pans, and other household utensils and furniture, they collect all their worn out clothes and other despicable things, sweep and cleanse their houses, squares, and the whole town, of their filth, which with all the remaining grain and other old provisions they cast together into one common heap, and consume it with fire. After having taken medicine, and fasted for three days, all the fire in the town is extinguished. During this fast they abstain from the gratification of every appetite and passion whatever. A general amnesty is proclaimed; all malefactors may return to their town."

"On the fourth morning, the high priest, by rubbing dry wood together, produces new fire in the public square, from whence every habitation in the town is supplied with the new and pure flame."

They then feast on the new corn and fruits, and dance and sing for three days, "and the four following days they receive visits and rejoice with their friends from neighboring towns who have in like manner purified and prepared themselves."

The Mexicans also practised a similar purification at the end of every fifty-two years, in the belief that it was time for the world to come to an end.

I have scarcely heard of a truer sacrament, that is, as the dictionary defines it, "outward and visible sign of an inward and spiritual grace," than this, and I have no doubt that they were originally inspired directly from Heaven to do thus, though they have no Biblical record of the revelation.

*

For more than five years I maintained myself thus solely by the labor of my hands, and I found that, by working about six weeks in a year, I could meet all the expenses of living. The whole of my winters, as well as most of my summers, I had free and clear for study. I have thoroughly tried schoolkeeping, and found that my expenses were in proportion, or rather out of proportion, to my income, for I was obliged to dress and train, not to say think and believe, accordingly, and I lost my time in the bargain. As I did not teach for the good of my fellow-men, but simply for a livelihood, this was a failure. I have tried trade but I found that it would take ten years to get under way in that, and that then I should probably be on my way to the devil. I was actually afraid that I might by that time be doing what is called a good business. When formerly I was looking about to see what I could do for a living, some sad experience in conforming to the wishes of friends being fresh in my mind to tax my ingenuity, I thought often and seriously of picking huckleberries: that surely I could do, and its small profits might suffice, — for my greatest skill has been to want but little, — so little capital it required, so little distraction from my wonted moods, I foolishly thought. While my acquaintances went unhesitatingly into trade or profession, I contemplated this occupation as most like theirs: ranging the hills all summer to pick the berries which came in my way, and thereafter carelessly dispose of them: so, to keep the flocks of Admetus. I also dreamed that I might gather the wild herbs, or carry evergreens to such villagers as loved to be reminded of the woods, even to the city, by hay-cart loads. But I have since learned that trade curses everything it handles; and though you trade in messages from heaven, the whole curse of trade attached to the business.

As I preferred some things to others, and especially valued my freedom, as I could fare hard and yet succeed well, I did not wish to spend my time in earning rich carpets or other fine furniture, or delicate cookery, or a house in the Grecian or Gothic style just yet. If there are any to whom it is no interruption to acquire these things, and who know how to use them when acquired, I relinquish to them the pursuit. Some are "industrious," and appear to love labor for its own sake, or perhaps because it keeps them out of worse mischief; to such I have at present nothing to say. Those who would not know what to do with more leisure than they now enjoy, I might advise to work twice as hard as they do, — work till they pay for themselves, and get their free papers. For myself I found that the occupation of a day-laborer was the most independent of any, especially as it required only thirty or forty days in a year to support one. The laborer's day ends with the going down of the sun, and he is then free to devote himself to his chosen pursuit, independent of his labor; but his employer, who speculates from month to month, has no respite from one end of the year to the other.

In short, I am convinced, both by faith and experience, that to maintain one's self on this earth is not a hardship but a pastime, if we will live simply and wisely; as the pursuits of the simpler nations are still the sports of the more artificial. It is not necessary that a man should earn his living by the sweat of his brow, unless he sweats easier than I do.

One young man of my acquaintance, who has inherited some acres, told me that he thought he should live as I did, *if he had the means.* I would not have any one adopt my mode of living on any account; for, beside that before he has fairly learned it I may have found out another for myself, I desire that there may be as many different persons in the world as possible; but I would have each one be very careful to find out and pursue *his own way,* and not his father's or his mother's or his neighbor's instead. The youth may build or plant or sail, only let him not be hindered from doing that which he tells me he would like to do. It is by a mathematical point only that we are wise, as the sailor or the fugitive slave keeps the polestar in his eye; but that is sufficient guidance for all our life. We may not arrive at our port within a calculable period, but we would preserve the true course.

*

I went to the woods because I wished to live deliberately, to front only the essential facts of life, and see if I could not learn what it had to teach, and not, when I came to die, discover that I had not lived. I did not wish to live what was not life, living is so dear; nor did I wish to practice resignation, unless it was quite necessary. I wanted to live deep and suck out all the marrow of life, to live so sturdily and Spartan-like as to put to rout all that was not life, to cut a broad swath and shave close, to drive life into a corner, and reduce it to its lowest terms, and, if it proved to be mean, why then to get the whole and genuine meanness of it, and publish its meanness to the world; or if it were sublime, to know it by experience, and be able to give a true account of it in my next excursion. For most men, it appears to me, are in a strange uncertainty about it, whether it is of the devil or of God, and have *somewhat hastily* concluded that it is the chief end of man here to "glorify God and enjoy him forever."

Still we live meanly, like ants; though the fable tells us that we were long ago changed into men; like pygmies we fight with cranes; it is error upon error, and clout upon clout, and our best virtue has for its occasion a superfluous and evitable wretchedness. Our life is frittered away by detail. An honest man has hardly need to count more than his ten fingers, or in extreme cases he may add his ten toes, and lump the rest. Simplicity, simplicity, simplicity! I say, let your affairs be a two or three, and not a hundred or a thousand; instead of a million count half a dozen, and keep your accounts on your thumb-nail. In the midst of this chopping sea of civilized life, such are the clouds and storms and quicksands and thousand-and-one items to be allowed for, that a man has to live, if he would not founder and go to the bottom and not make his port at all, by dead reckoning, and he must be a great calculator indeed who succeeds. Simplify, simplify. Instead of three meals a day, if it be necessary eat but one; instead of a hundred dishes, five; and reduce other things in proportion. Our life is like a German Confederacy, made up of petty states, with its boundary forever fluctuating, so that even a German cannot tell you how it is bounded at any moment. The nation itself, with all its so-called internal improvements, which, by the way are all external and superficial, is just such an unwieldy and overgrown establishment, cluttered with furniture and tripped up by its own traps, ruined by luxury and heedless expense, by want of calculation and a worthy aim, as the million households in the land; and the only cure for it, as for them, is in a rigid economy, a stern and more than Spartan simplicity of life and elevation of purpose. It lives too fast. Men think that it is essential that the *Nation* have commerce, and export ice, and talk through a telegraph, and ride thirty miles an hour, without a doubt, whether *they* do or not; but whether we should live like baboons or like men, is a little uncertain. If we do not get out sleepers, and forge rails, and devote days and nights to the work, but go to tinkering upon our *lives* to improve *them*, who will build railroads? And if railroads are not built, how shall we get to heaven in a season? But if we stay at home and mind our business, who will want railroads? We do not ride on the railroad; it rides upon us. Did you ever think what those sleepers are that underlie the railroad? Each one is a man, an Irishman, or a Yankee man. The rails are laid on them, and they are covered with sand, and the cars run smoothly over them. They are sound sleepers, I assure you. And every few years a new lot is laid down and run over; so that, if some have the pleasure of riding on a rail, others have the misfortune to be ridden upon. And when they run over a man that is walking in his sleep, a supernumerary sleeper in the wrong position, and wake him up, they suddenly stop the cars, and make a hue and cry about it, as if this were an exception. I am glad to know that it takes a gang of men for every five miles to keep the sleepers down and level in their beds as it is, for this is a sign that they may sometime get up again.

*

Shams and delusions are esteemed for soundest truths, while reality is fabulous. If men would steadily observe realities only, and not allow themselves to be deluded, life, to compare it with such things as we know, would be like a fairy tale and the Arabian Nights' Entertainments. If we respect only what is inevitable and has a right to be, music and poetry would resound along the streets. When we are unhurried and wise, we percieve that only great and worthy things have any permanent and absolute existence, that petty fears and petty pleasures are but the shadow of the reality. This is always exhilarating and sublime. By closing the eyes and slumbering, and consenting to be deceived by shows, men establish and confirm their daily life of routine and habit everywhere, which still is built on purely illusory foundations. Children, who play life, discern its true law and relations more clearly than men, who fail to live it worthily, but who think that they are wiser by

The Self as Awareness

experience, that is, by failure. I have read in a Hindoo book, that "there was a king's son, who, being expelled in infancy from his native city, was brought up by a forester, and, growing up to maturity in that state, imagined himself to belong to the barbarous race with which he lived. One of his father's ministers having discovered him, revealed to him what he was, and the misconception of his character was removed, and he knew himself to be a prince. So soul," continues the Hindoo philosopher, "from the circumstances in which it is placed, mistakes its own character, until the truth is revealed to it by some holy teacher, and then it knows itself to be *Brahme*." I perceive that we inhabitants of New England live this mean life that we do because our vision does not penetrate the surface of things. We think that that *is* which *appears* to be. If a man should walk through this town and see only the reality, where, think you, would the "Mill-dam" go to? If he should give us an account of the realities he beheld there, we should not recognize the place in his description. Look at a meeting-house, or a court-house, or a jail, or a shop, or a dwelling-house, and say what that thing is before a true gaze, and they would all go to pieces in your account of them. Men esteem truth remote, in the outskirts of the system, behind the farthest star, before Adam and after the last man. In eternity there is indeed something true and sublime. But all these times and places and occasions are now and here. God himself culminates in the present moment, and will never be more divine in the lapse of all the ages. And we are enabled to apprehend at all what is sublime and noble only by the perpetual instilling and drenching of the reality that surrounds us. The universe constantly and obediently answers to our conceptions; whether we travel fast or slow, the track is laid for us. Let us spend our lives in conceiving then. The poet or the artist never yet had so fair and noble a design but some of his posterity at least could accomplish it.

*

My residence was more favorable, not only to thought, but to serious reading, than a university; and though I was beyond the range of the ordinary circulating library, I had more than ever come within the influence of those books which circulate round the world, whose sentences were first written on bark, and are not merely copied from time to time on to linen paper. Says the poet Mîr Camar Uddîn Mast, "Being seated, to run through the region of the spiritual world; I have had this advantage in books. To be intoxicated by a single glass of wine; I have experienced this pleasure when I have drunk the liquor of the esoteric doctrines." I kept Homer's Illiad on my table through the summer, though I looked at his page only now and then. Incessant labor with my hands, at first, for I had my house to finish and my beans to hoe at the same time, made more study impossible. Yet I sustained myself by the prospect of such reading in future. I read one or two shallow books of travel in the intervals of my work, till that employment made me ashamed of myself, and I asked where it was then that I lived.

*

The works of the great poets have never yet been read by mankind, for only great poets can read them. They have only been read as the multitude read the stars, at most astrologically, not astronomically. Most men have learned to read to serve a paltry convenience, a they have learned to cipher in order to keep accounts and not be cheated in trade; but of reading as a noble intellectual exercise they know little or nothing; yet this only is reading, in a high sense, not that which lulls us as a luxury and suffers the nobler faculties to sleep the while, but what we have to stand on tip-toe to read and devote our most alert and wakeful hours to.

*

I aspire to be acquainted with wiser men than this our Concord soil has produced, whose names are hardly known here. Or shall I hear the name of Plato and never read his book? As if Plato were my townsman and I never saw him,—my next neighbor and I never heard him speak or attended to the wisdom of his words. But how actually is it? His Dialogues, which contain what was immortal in him, lie on the next shelf, and yet I never read them. We are underbred and lowlived and illiterate; and in this respect I confess I do not make any very broad distinction between the illiterateness of my townsmen who cannot read at all and the illiterateness of him who has learned to read only what is for children and feeble intellects. We should be as good as the worthies of antiquity, but partly by first knowing how good they were. We are a race of tit-men, and soar but little higher in our intellectual flights than the columns of the daily paper.

*

We boast that we belong to the Nineteenth Century and are making the most rapid strides of any nation. But consider how little this village does for its own culture. I do not wish to flatter my townsmen, nor to be flattered by them, for that will not advance either of us. We need to be provoked,—goaded like oxen, as we are, into a trot. We have a comparatively decent system of common schools, schools for infants only; but excepting the half-starved Lyceum in the winter, and latterly the puny beginning of a library suggested by the State, no schools for ourselves. We spend more on almost any article of bodily ailment than on our mental ailment. It is time that we had uncommon schools, that we did not leave off our education when we begin to be men and women. It is time that villages were universities, and their elder inhabitants the fellows of universities, with leisure—if they are, indeed, so well off—to pursue liberal studies the rest of their lives. Shall the world be confined to one Paris or one Oxford forever? Cannot students be boarded here and get a liberal education under the skies of Concord? Can we not hire some Abélard to lecture to us? Alas! what with foddering the cattle and tending the store, we are kept from school too long, and our education is sadly neglected. In this country, the village should in some respects take the place of the nobleman of Europe. It should be the patron of the fine arts. It is rich enough. It wants only the magnanimity and refinement. It can spend money enough on such things as farmer's and trader's value, but it is thought Utopian to propose spending money for things which more intelligent men know to be of far more worth. This town has spent seventeen thousand dollars on a town-house, thank fortune or politics, but probably it will not spend so much on living wit, the true meat to put into that shell, in a hundred years. The one hundred and twenty-five dollars annually subscribed for a Lyceum in the winter is better spent than any other equal sum raised in the town. If we live in the Nineteenth Century, why should we not enjoy the advantages which the Nineteenth Century offers? Why should our life be in any respect provincial? If we read newspapers, why not skip the gossip of Boston and take the best newspaper in the world at once?—not be sucking the pap of "neutral family" papers, or browsing "Olive-Branches" here in New England. Let the reports of all the learned societies come to us, and we will see if they know anything. Why should we leave it to Harper & Brothers and Redding & Co. to select our reading? As the nobleman of cultivated taste surrounds himself with whatever conduces to his culture, — genius — learning — wit — books — paintings — statuary — music — philosophical instruments, and the like; so let the village do, — not stop short at a pedagogue, a parson, a sexton, a parish library, and three select-men, because our Pilgrim forefathers got through a cold winter once on a bleak rock with these. To act collectively is according to the spirit of our institutions; and I am confident that, as our circumstances are more flourishing, our means are greater than the nobleman's. New England can hire all the wise men in the world to come and teach her, and board them round the while, and not be provincial at all. That is the *uncommon* school we want. Instead of noblemen, let us have noble villages of men. If it is necessary, omit one bridge over the river, go round a little there, and throw one arch at least over the darker gulf of ignorance which surrounds us.

William Wordsworth:
"The World Is Too Much With Us"

Wordsworth (1770-1850) studied at Cambridge University, refused to embark on a regular career, spent time in France during the years of the Revolution, and then spent the greater part of his life in the English countryside. As a young man he became an admirer of the French Revolution and its ideals, but then became gradually disillusioned. When Napolean rose to power, Wordsworth became an ardent English patriot.

During the years of 1797-1798 Wordsworth, his sister Dorothy, and Samuel T. Coleridge had a period of intensive friendship. They travelled together to Germany to study that country's literature and philosophy (but only Coleridge followed through with this plan). After this period, Wordsworth's external life became rather uneventful. For a decade or so he produced his most important poetical work, with the intensive experience of nature as its main theme. His remaining years were characterized by waning creative power, growing conservatism, and slowly growing fame.

The following sonnet deplores the fact that all our time, energy, and attention is absorbed by the mundane preoccupations of what constitutes everyday life in Western civilization. Wordsworth suggests that this impoverishes us by cutting us off from the real sources of life, nature. His lament fits in with the observations of critics of our contemporary way of life. The basic perception is that humans have become the masters of nature as never before, but that they are also deeply alienated from what they rule, and that they have become in themselves unimaginative and emotionally dead.

The world is too much with us: late and soon,
Getting and spending. we lay waste our powers:
Little we see in Nature that is ours;

We have given our hearts away, a sordid boon!
The sea that bares her bosom to the moon;
The winds that will be howling at all hours,
And are up-gathered now like sleeping flowers;
For this, for everything, we are out of tune;
It moves us not. — Great God! I'd rather be
A Pagan suckled in a creed outworn;
So might I, standing on this pleasant lea,
Have glimpses that would make me less forlorn;
Have sight of Proteus rising from the sea;
Or hear old Triton blow his wreathed horn.

Angelus Silesius: "You Are Your Own Prison"

The Latin name Angelus Silesius was taken by Johannes Scheffler (1624-1677) on his conversion to Catholicism. His short, concentrated poems are counted among the great mystical writings of the West. The following epigram can serve as a reminder that human self-alienation is not only a fate brought about by external forces, but is also rooted in and maintained by our own attitudes, values, and experiences.

The world will hold you not, you yourself are the world
That holds you in yourself so fast.

Walt Whitman: "One's-Self I Sing"

There is a tendency to think in exclusive categories, in terms of antagonistic cliches, in the spirit of sectarianism. Thoreau as an individualist is pitted against Marx the mass agitator, the sensuous person against the intellectual, the male against the female, Europe against America, the West against the Orient, and so forth. And along with this thinking go claims of allegiance, of tight adherence to either/or. It should not be denied that the above distinctions are often meaningful and useful, and that in certain situations it testifies to fuzzy thinking if such distinctions are not perceived. But such distinctions are tied to specific contexts; they cannot be understood as absolutes, or value-laden dogmas. More often than not, two alternative descriptions turn out to be just two aspects of the same thing.

Such categorical flexibility is advocated in the following poem. For Whitman the truth of life cannot be grasped in isolated and isolating sections, but only in its immense wholeness. A fully developed self can never be sectarian, but only one that is open to the whole of life. (And that includes, as Whitman says in other places, death as well.)

One's-Self I sing, a simple, separate person,
Yet utter the word Democratic, the word En-masse.

Of physiology from top to toe I sing;
Not physiognomy alone nor brain alone is worthy of the
    Muse, I say the Form complete is worthier far,
The Female equally with the Male I sing.

Of Life immense in passion, pulse, and power,
Cheerful, for freest action form'd under the laws divine,
The Modern Man I sing.

8. Looking Beyond the Known World

XII. THE SELF AS FLUX

SELF DETERMINATION

Ralph W. Emerson: "Self Reliance"

AUTHOR AND TEXT: *Ralph Waldo Emerson (1803-1882) was the leading writer and thinker of the New England Transcendentalists. Transcendentalism was a philosophical and literary movement which flourished in New England during the decades before the Civil War. Its major philosophical conviction was that genuine human knowledge does not come from passively receiving sense impressions and social indoctrination, but originates from the creative intuitions of all individuals. One of the major influences on this philosophy was the philosophy of Immanuel Kant, which Emerson knew primarily through the works of Coleridge and Carlyle.*

Throughout Emerson's writings there is an emphasis on self-reliance. "There is really nothing external, I must spin my thread from my own bowels," and "the purpose of life seems to be to acquaint a man with himself" sums up the direction of his thought.

Emerson's emphasis on self-reliance, his critique of a society which accepts conventional wisdom too blindly, made him many enemies. Conservatives in New England liked his ideas as little as the German authorities liked those of their Critical Philosophers. When Emerson gave his famous address to the Harvard Divinity School, e.g., he provoked such strong hostilities that he was not asked to come back for thirty years—by which time he had become America's best known man of letters.

"Self-Reliance," from which the following selections are taken, was published in 1841.

SELF AND CARING FOR OTHERS: *Emerson's remarks against charitable institutions may sound crudely egoistic. It should be noticed, however, that Emerson does not argue for the philosophy of Social Darwinism which glorifies the war of all against all, and the resulting survival of the "fittest." Indeed, Emerson does not argue against a social organization in which all members are autonomous and equal, and in which charity for able-bodied persons would not be necessary in the first place. Emerson's concern with charity is with its crippling effects on giver and receiver. People who are taken care of by others are in danger of turning into passive, manipulable objects without either freedom or responsibility. People who take care of others are in danger of not living their own lives, of living substitute lives through others, often acting on their bad conscience (Super-Ego) rather than out of genuine compassion and solidarity.*

INSTINCT AND REASON: *In describing intuition and instinct as the real center of every person, Emerson (as little as Nietzsche or Freud) does not argue against the use of reason, intelligent behaviour, etc. Emerson is not an anti-intellectual. His point is to forestall the kind of spurious intellectual life which functions as a substitute life, while allowing the supression and underdevelopment of the physical and emotional nature of mankind.*

~ ~ ~

I read the other day some verses written by an eminent painter which were original and not conventional. The soul always hears an admonition in such lines, let the subject be what it may. The sentiment they instill is of more value than any thought they may contain. To believe your own thought, to believe that what is true for you in your private heart is true for all men,—that is genius. Speak your latent conviction, and it shall be the universal sense; for the inmost in due time becomes the outmost, and our first thought is rendered back to us by the trumpets of the Last Judgment. Familiar as the voice of the mind is to each, the highest merit we ascribe to Moses, Plato and Milton is that they set at naught books and traditions, and spoke not what men, but what they thought. A man should learn to detect and watch that gleam of light which flashes across his mind from within, more than the lustre of the firmament of bards and sages. Yet he dismisses without notice his thought, because it is his. In every work of genius we recognize our own rejected thoughts; they come back to us with a certain alienated majesty. Great works of art have no more affecting lesson for us than this. They teach us to abide by our spontaneous impression with good-humored inflexibility then most when the whole cry of voices is on the other side. Else to-morrow a stranger will say with masterly good sense precisely what we have thought and felt all the time, and we shall be forced to take with shame our own opinion from another.

*

Trust thyself; every heart vibrates to that iron string. Accept the place the divine providence has found for you, the society of your contemporaries, the connection of events. Great men have always done so, and confided themselves childlike to the genius of their age, betraying their perception that the absolutely trustworthy was seated at their heart, working through their hands, predominating in all their being. And we are now men, and must accept in the highest mind the same transcendent destiny; and not minors and invalids in a protected corner, not cowards fleeing before a revolution, but guides, redeemers and benefactors, obeying the Almighty effort and advancing on Chaos and the Dark.

*

The nonchalance of boys who are sure of a dinner, and would disdain as much as a lord to do or say aught to conciliate one, is the healthy attitude of human nature. A boy is in the parlor what the pit is in the playhouse: independent, irresponsible, looking out from his corner on such people and facts as pass by, he tries and sentences them on their merits, in the swift, summary way of boys, as good, bad, interesting, silly, eloquent, troublesome. He cumbers himself never about consequences, about interests; he gives an independent, genuine verdict. You must court him; he does not court you. But the man is as it were clapped into jail by his consciousness. As soon as he has once acted or spoken with eclat he is a committed person, watched by the sympathy or the hatred of hundreds, whose affections must now enter into his account. There is no Lethe for this. Ah, that he could pass again into his neutrality! Who can thus avoid all pledges and, having observed, observes again from the same unaffected, unbiased, unbribable, unaffrighted innocence,—must always be formidable. He would utter opinions on all passing affairs, which being seen to be not private but necessary, would sink like darts into the ear of men and put them in fear.

These are the voices which we hear in solitude, but they grow faint and inaudible as we enter into the world. Society everywhere is in conspiracy against the manhood of every one of its members. Society is a joint-stock company, in which the members agree, for the better securing of his bread to each shareholder, to surrender the liberty and culture of the eater. The virtue in most request is conformity. Self-reliance is its aversion. It loves not realities and creators, but names and customs.

Whoso would be a man, must be a nonconformist. He who would gather immortal palms must not be hindered by the name of goodness, but must explore if it be goodness. Nothing is at last sacred but the integrity of your own mind. Absolve you to yourself, and you shall have the suffrage of the world. I remember an answer which when quite young I was prompted to make to a valued adviser who was wont to importune me with the dear old doctrines of the church. On my saying, "What have I to do with the sacredness of traditions, if I live wholly from within?" my friend suggested—"But these impulses may be from below, not from above." I replied, "They do not seem to me to be such; but if I am the Devil's child, I will live then from the Devil." No law can be sacred to me but that of my nature. Good and bad are but names very readily transferable to that or this; the only right is what is after my constitution; the only wrong what is against it. A man is to carry himself in the presence of all opposition as if every thing were titular and ephemeral but he. I am ashamed to think how easily we capitulate to badges and names, to large societies and dead institutions. Every decent and well-spoken individual affects and sways me more than is right. I ought to go upright and vital, and speak the rude truth in all ways. If malice and vanity wear the coat of philanthropy, shall that pass? If an angry bigot assumes this bountiful cause of Abolition, and comes to me with his last news from Barbadoes, why should I not say to him, 'Go love thy infant; love the wood-chopper;

be good-natured and modest; have that grace; and never varnish your hard, uncharitable ambition with this incredible tenderness for black folk a thousand miles off. Thy love afar is spite at home.' Rough and graceless would be such greeting, but truth is handsomer than the affectation of love. Your goodness must have some edge to it, — else it is none. The doctrine of hatred must be preached, as the counteraction of the doctrine of love, when that pulses and whines. I shun father and mother and wife and brother when my genius calls me. I would write on the lintels of the doorpost, Whim. I hope it is somewhat better than whim at last, but we cannot spend the day in explanation. Expect me not to show cause why I seek or why I exclude company. Then again, do not tell me, as a good man did to-day, of my obligation to put all poor men in good situations. Are they my poor? I tell thee thou foolish philanthropist that I grudge the dollar, the dime, the cent I give to such men as do not belong to me and to whom I do not belong. There is a class of persons to whom by all spiritual affinity I am bought and sold; for them I will go to prison if need be, but your miscellaneous popular charities; the education at college of fools; the building of meeting-houses to the vain end to which many now stand; alms to sots, and the thousand-fold Relief Societies; — though I confess with shame I sometimes succumb and give the dollar, it is a wicked dollar, which by and by I shall have the manhood to withhold.

Virtues are, in the popular estimate, rather the exception than the rule. There is the man and his virtues. Men do what is called a good action, as some piece of courage or charity, much as they would pay a fine in expiation of daily non-appearance on parade. Their works are done as an apology or extenuation of their living in the world, — as invalids and the insane pay a high board. Their virtues are penances. I do not wish to expiate, but to live. My life is for itself and not for a spectacle. I much prefer that it should be of a lower strain, so it be genuine and equal, than that it should be glittering and unsteady. I wish it to be sound and sweet, and not to need diet and bleeding. I ask primary evidence that you are a man, and refuse this appeal from the man to his actions. I know that for myself it makes no difference whether I do or forbear those actions which are reckoned excellent. I cannot consent to pay for a privilege where I have intrinsic right. Few and mean as my gifts may be, I actually am, and do not need for my own assurance or the assurance of my fellows any secondary testimony.

What I must do is all that concerns me, not what the people think. This rule, equally arduous in actual and in intellectual life, may serve for the whole distinction between greatness and meanness. It is the harder because you will always find those who think they know what is your duty better than you know it. It is easy in the world to live after our own; but the great man is he who in the midst of the crowd keeps with perfect sweetness the independence of solitude.

The objection to conforming to usages that have become dead to you is that it scatters your force. It loses your time and blurs the impression of your character. If you maintain a dead church, contribute to a dead Bible-society, vote with a great party either for the government or against it, spread your table like base housekeepers,—under all these screens I have difficulty to detect the precise man you are: and of course so much force is withdrawn from your proper life. But do your work, and I shall know you. Do your work, and you shall reinforce yourself. A man must consider what a blindman's-buff is this game of conformity. If I know your sect I anticipate your argument. I hear a preacher announce for his text and topic in the expediency of one of the institutions of his church. Do I not know beforehand that not possibly can he say a new and spontaneous word? Do I not know beforehand that with all this ostentation of examining the grounds of the institution he will do no such thing? Do I not know that he is pledged to himself, not to look but at one side, the permitted side, not as a man, but as a parish minister? He is a retained attorney, and these airs of the bench are the emptiest affectation. Well, most men have bound their eyes with one or another handkerchief, and attached themselves to some one of these communities of opinion. This conformity makes them not false in a few particulars, authors of a few lies, but false in all particulars. Their every truth is not quite true. Their two is not the real two, their four not the real four; so that every word they say chagrins us and we know not where to begin to set them right. Meantime nature is not slow to equip us in the prison-uniform of the party to which we adhere. We come to wear one cut of face and figure, and acquire by degrees the gentlest asinine expression. There is a mortifying experience in particular, which does not fail to wreak itself also in the general history; I mean "the foolish face of praise," the forced smile which we put on in company where we do not feel at ease, in answer to conversation which does not interest us. The muscles, not spontaneously moved but moved by a low usurping wilfulness, grow tight about the outline of the face, with the most disagreeable sensation.

For nonconformity the world whips you with its displeasure. And therefore a man must know how to estimate a sour face. The by-standers look askance on him in the public street or in the friend's parlor. If this aversion had its origin in contempt and resistance like his own he might well go home with a sad countenance; but the sour faces of the multitude, like their sweet faces, have no deep cause, but are put on and off as the wind blows and a newspaper directs. Yet is the discontent of the multitude more formidable than that of the senate and the college? It is easy enough for a firm man who knows the world to brook the rage of the cultivated classes. Their rage is decorous and prudent, for they are timid, as being very vulnerable themselves. But when to their feminine rage the indignation of the people is added, when the ignorant and the poor are aroused, when the unintelligent brute force that lies at the bottom of society is made to growl and mow, it needs the habit of magnanimity and religion to treat it godlike as a trifle of no concernment.

The other terror that scares us from self-trust is our consistency: a reverence for our past act or word because the eyes of others have no other data for computing our orbit than our past acts, and we are loath to disappoint them.

But why should you keep your head over your shoulder? Why drag about this corpse of your memory, lest you contradict somewhat you have stated in this or that public place? Suppose you should contradict yourself; what then? It seems to be a rule of wisdom never to rely on your memory alone, scarcely even in acts of pure memory, but to bring the past for judgment into the thousand-eyed present, and live ever in a new day. In your metaphysics you have denied personality to the Deity, yet when the devout motions of the soul come, yield to them heart and life, though they should clothe God with shape and color. Leave your theory, as Joseph his coat in the hand of the harlot, and flee.

A foolish consistency is the hobgoblin of little minds, adored by little statesmen and philosophers and divines. With consistency a great soul has simply nothing to do. He may as well concern himself with his shadow on the wall. Speak what you think now in hard words again, though it contradict every thing you said to-day. — 'Ah, so you shall be sure to be misunderstood.' — Is it so bad then to be misunderstood? Pythagoras was misunderstood, and Socrates, and Jesus, and Luther, and Copernicus, and Galileo, and Newton, and every pure and wise spirit that ever took flesh. To be great is to be misunderstood.

I suppose no man can violate his nature. All the sallies of his will are rounded in by the law of his being, as the inequalities of Andes and Himalaya are insignificant in the curve of the sphere. Nor does it matter how you gauge and try him. A character is like an acrostic or Alexandrian stanza; — read it forward, backward, or across, it still spells the same thing. In this pleasing contrite wood-life which God allows me, let me record day by day my honest thought without prospect or retrospect, and, I cannot doubt, it will be found symmetrical, though I mean it not and see it not. My book should smell of pines and resound with the hum of insects. The swallow over my window should interweave that thread or straw he carries in his bill into my web also. We pass for what we are. Character teaches above our wills. Men imagine that they communicate their virtue or vice only by overt actions, and do not see that virtue or vice emit a breath every moment.

There will be an agreement in whatever variety of actions, so they be each honest and natural in their hour. For of one will, the actions will be harmonious, however unlike they seem. These varieties are lost sight of at a little distance, at a little height of thought. One tendency unites them all. The voyage of the best ship is a zigzag line of a hundred tacks. See the line from a sufficient distance, and it straightens itself to the average tendency. Your genuine action will explain itself and will explain your other genuine actions. Your conformity explains nothing. Act singly, and what you have already done singly will justify you now. Greatness appeals to the future. If I can be firm enough to-day to do right and scorn eyes, I must have done so much right before as to defend me now. Be it how it will, do right now. Always scorn appearances and you always may. The force of character is cumulative. All the foregone days of virtue work their health into this. What makes the majesty of the heroes of the senate and the field, which so fills the imagination? The consciousness of a train of great days and victories behind. They shed a united light on the advancing actor. He is attended as by a visible escort of angels. That is it which throws thunder into Chatlan's voice, and dignity into Washington's port, and America into Adam's eye. Honor is venerable to us because it is no ephemera. It is always ancient virtue. We worship it to-day because it is not of to-day. We love it and pay it homage because it is not a trap for our love and homage, but is self-dependent, self-derived, and therefore of an old immaculate pedigree, even if shown in a young person.

I hope in these days we have heard the last of conformity and consistency. Let the words be gazetted and ridiculous henceforward. Instead of the gong for dinner, let us hear a whistle from the Spartan fife. Let us never bow and apologize more. A great man is coming to eat at my house. I do not wish to please him; I wish that he should wish to please me. . .

*

The magnetism which all original action exerts is explained when we inquire the reason of self-trust. Who is the Trustee? What is the aboriginal Self, on which a universal reliance may be grounded? What is the nature and power of that science-baffling star, without parallax, without calculable elements, which shoots a ray of beauty even into trivial and impure actions, if the least mark of independence appear? The inquiry leads us to that source, at once the essence of genius, of virtue, and of life, which we call Spontaneity or Instinct. We denote this primary wisdom as Intuition, whilst all later teachings are tuitions. In that deep force, the last fact behind which analysis cannot go, all things find their common origin.

*

The relations of the soul to the divine spirit are so pure that it is profane to seek to interpose helps. It must be that when God speaketh he should communicate, not one thing, but all things; should fill the world with his voice; should scatter forth light, nature, time, souls, from the centre of the present thought; and new date and new create the whole. Whenever a mind is simple and receives a divine wisdom, old things pass away, — means, teachers, texts, temples fall; it lives now, and absorbs past and future into the present hour. All things are made sacred by relation to it, — one as much as another. All things are dissolved to their centre by their cause, and in the universal miracle petty and particular miracles disappear. If therefore a man claims to know and speak of God and carries you backward to the phraseology of some old mouldered nation in another world, believe him not. Is the acorn better than the oak which is its fulness and completion? Is the parent better than the child into whom he has cast his ripened being? Whence then this worship of the past? The centuries are conspirators against the sanity and authority of the soul. Time and space are but physiological colors which the eye makes, but the soul is light: where it is, is day; where it was, is night; and history is an impertinence and an injury if it be anything more than a cheerful apologue or parable of my being and becoming.

Man is timid and apologetic; he is no longer upright; he dares not say 'I think,' 'I am,' but quotes some saint or sage. He is ashamed before the blade of grass or the blowing rose. These roses under my window make no reference to former roses or to better ones; they are for what they are; they exist with God to-day. There is no time to them. There is simply the rose; it is perfect in every moment of its existence. Before a leaf-bud has burst, its whole life acts; in the full-blown flower there is no more; in the leafless root there is no more; in the leafless root there is no less. Its nature is satisfied and it satisfies nature in all moments alike. But man postpones or remembers; he does not live in the present, but with reverted eye laments the past, or, heedless of the riches that surround him, stands on tiptoe to foresee the future. He cannot be happy and strong until he too lives with nature in the present, above time.

This should be plain enough. Yet see what strong intellects dare not yet hear God himself unless he speak the phraseology of I know not what David, or Jeremiah, or Paul. We shall not always set so great a price on a few texts, on a few lives. We are like children who repeat by rote the sentences of grandames and tutors, and, as they grow older, of the men of talents and character they chance to see, — painfully recollecting the exact words they spoke; afterwards, when they come into the point of view which those had who uttered these sayings, they understand them and are willing to let the words go; for at any time they can use words as good when occasion comes. If we live truly, we shall see truly. It is as easy for the strong man to be strong, as it is for the weak to be weak. When we have new perception, we shall gladly disburden the memory of its hoarded treasures as old rubbish. When a man lives with God, his voice shall be as sweet as the murmur of the brook and the rustle of the corn.

And now at last the highest truth on this subject remains unsaid; probably cannot be said; for all that we say is the far-off remembering of the intuition. That thought by what I can now nearest approach to say it, is this. When good is near you, when you have life in yourself, it is not by any known or accustomed way; you shall not discern the footprints of any other; — the way, the thought, the good, shall be wholly strange and new. It shall exclude example and experience. You take the way from man, not to man. All persons that ever existed are its forgotten ministers. Fear and hope are alike beneath it. There is somewhat low even in hope. In the hour of vision there is nothing that can be called gratitude, nor properly joy. The soul raised over passion beholds identity and eternal causation, perceives the self-existence of Truth and Right, and calms itself with knowing that all things go well. Vast spaces of nature, the Atlantic Ocean, the South Sea; long intervals of time, years, centuries, are of no account. This which I think and feel underlay every former state of life and circumstances, as it does underlie my present, and what is called life and what is called death.

Life only avails, not the having lived. Power ceases in the instant of repose; it resides in the moment of transition from a past to a new state, in the shooting of the gulf, in the darting to an aim. This one fact the world hates; that the soul becomes; for that forever degrades the past, turns all riches to poverty, all reputation to a shame, confounds the saint with the rogue, shoves Jesus and Judas equally aside.

*

But now we are a mob. Man does not stand in awe of man, nor is his genius admonished to stay at home, to put itself in communication with the internal ocean, but it goes abroad to beg a cup of water of the urns of other men. We must go alone. I like the silent church before the service begins, better than the preaching. How far off, how cool, how chaste the persons look, begirt each one with a precinct or sanctuary! So let us always sit. Why should we assume the faults of our friend, or wife, or father, or child, because they sit around our hearth, or are said to have the same blood? All men have my blood and I have all men's. Not for that will I adopt their petulance or folly, even to the extent of being ashamed of it. But your isolation must not be mechanical, but spiritual, that is, must be elevation. At times the whole world seems to be in conspiracy to importune you with emphatic trifles. Friend, client, child, sickness, fear, want, charity, all knock at once at thy closet door and say,—'Come out unto us.' But keep thy state; come not into their confusion. The power men possess to annoy me I give them by a weak curiosity. No man can come near me but through my act. "What we love that we have, but by desire we bereave ourselves of the love."

If we cannot at once rise to the sanctities of obedience and faith, let us at least resist our temptations; let us enter into the state of war and wake Thor and Woden, courage and constancy, in our Saxon breasts. This is to be done in our smooth times by speaking the truth. Check this lying hospitality and lying affection. Live no longer to the expectation of these deceived and deceiving people with whom we converse. Say to them, 'O father, O mother, O wife, O brother, O friend, I have lived with you after appearances hitherto. Henceforward I am the truth's. Be it known unto you that henceforward I obey no law less than the eternal law. I will have no covenants but proximities. I shall endeavor to nourish parents, to support my family, to be the chaste husband of one wife,—but these relations I must fill after a new and unprecedented way. I appeal from your customs. I must be myself. I cannot break myself any longer for you, or you. If you can love me for what I am, we shall be the happier. If you cannot, I will still seek to deserve that you should. I will not hide my tastes or aversions. I will so trust that what is deep is holy, that I will do strongly before the sun and moon whatever only rejoices me and the heart appoints. If you are noble, I will love you; if you are not, I will not hurt you and myself by hypocritical attentions. If you are true, but not in the same truth with me, cleave to your companions; I will seek my own. I do this not selfishly but humbly and truly. It is alike your interest, and mine, and all men's, however long we have dwelt in lies, to live in truth. Does this sound harsh to-day? You will soon love what is dictated by your nature as well as mine, and if we follow the truth it will bring us out safe at last.'—But so may you give these friends pain. Yes, but I cannot sell my liberty and my power, to save their sensibility. Besides, all persons have their moments of reason, when they look out into the region of absolute truth; then will they justify me and do the same thing.

*

If any man consider the present aspects of what is called, by distinction, *society*, he will see the need of these ethics. The sinew and heart of man seem to be drawn out, and we are become timorous, desponding whimperers. We are afraid of truth, afraid of fortune, afraid of death and afraid of each other. Our age yields no great and perfect persons. We want men and women who shall renovate life and our social state, but we see that most natures are insolvent, cannot satisfy their own wants, have an ambition out of all proportion to their practical force and do lean and beg day and night continually. Our housekeeping is mendicant, our arts, our occupations, our marriages, our religion we have not chosen, but society has chosen for us. We shun the rugged battle of fate, where strength is born.

If our young men miscarry in their first enterprises they lose all heart. If the young merchant fails, men say he is ruined. If the finest genius studies at one of our colleges and is not installed in an office within one year afterwards in the cities or suburbs of Boston or New York, it seems to his friends and to himself that he is right in being disheartened and in complaining the rest of his life. A sturdy lad from New Hampshire or Vermont, who in turn tries all the professions, who teams it, farms it, peddles, keeps a school, preaches, edits a newspaper, goes to Congress, buys a township, and so forth, in successive years, and always like a cat falls on his feet, is worth a hundred of these city dolls. He walks abreast with his days and feels no shame in not 'studying a profession,' for he does not postpone his life, but lives already. He has not one chance, but a hundred chances. Let a Stoic open the resources of man and tell men they are not leaning willows, but can and must detach themselves; that with the exercise of self-trust, new powers shall appear; that a man is the word made flesh, born to shed healing to the nations; that he should be ashamed of our compassion, and that the moment he acts from himself, tossing the laws, the books, idolatries and customs out of the window; we pity him no more but thank and revere him;—and that teacher shall restore the life of man to splendor and make his name dear to all history.

It is easy to see that a greater self-reliance must work a revolution in all the offices and relations of men; in their religion; in their education; in their pursuits; their modes of living; their association; in their property; in their speculative views.

1. In what prayers do men allow themselves! That which they call a holy office is not so much as brave and manly. Prayer looks abroad and asks for some foreign addition to come through some foreign virtue, and loses itself in endless mazes of natural and supernatural, and mediatorial and miraculous. Prayer that craves a particular commodity, anything less than all good, is vicious. Prayer is the contemplation of the facts of life from the highest point of view. It is the soliloquy of a beholding and jubilant soul.

*

2. It is for want of self-culture that the superstition of Travelling, whose idols are Italy, England, Egypt, retains its fascination for all educated Americans. They who made England, Italy, or Greece venerable in the imagination, did so by sticking fast where they were, like an axis of the earth. In manly hours we feel that duty is our place. The soul is no traveller; the wise man stays at home, and when his necessities, his duties, on any occasion call him from his house, or into foreign lands, he is at home still and shall make men sensible by the expression of his countenance that he goes, the missionary of wisdom and virtue, and visits cities and men like a sovereign and not like an interloper or a valet.

I have no churlish objection to the circumnavigation of the globe for the purposes of art, of study, and benevolence, so that the man is first domesticated, or does not go abroad with the hope of finding somewhat greater than he knows. He who travels to be amused, or to get somewhat which he does not carry, travels away from himself, and grows old even in youth among old things. In Thebes, in Palmyra, his will and mind have become old and dilapidated as they. He carries ruins to ruins.

*

3. But the rage of travelling is a symptom of a deeper unsoundness affecting the whole intellectual action. The intellect is vagabond, and our system of education fosters restlessness. Our minds travel when our bodies are forced to stay at home. We imitate; and what is imitation but the

travelling of the mind? Our houses are built with foreign taste; our shelves are garnished with foreign ornaments; our opinions, our tastes, our faculties, lean, and follow the Past and the Distant. The soul created the arts wherever they have flourished. It was in his own mind that the artist sought his model. It was an application of his own thought to the thing to be done and the conditions to be observed. And why need we copy the Doric or the Gothic model? Beauty, convenience, grandeur of thought and quaint expression are as near to us as to any, and if the American artist will study with hope and love the precise thing to be done by him, considering the climate, the soil, the length of the day, the wants of the people, the habit and form of the government, he will create a house in which all these will find themselves fitted, and taste and sentiment will be satisfied also.

*

4. As our Religion, our Education, our Art look abroad, so does our spirit of society. All men plume themselves on the improvement of society, and no man improves.

Society never advances. It recedes as fast on one side as it gains on the other. It undergoes continual changes; it is barbarous, it is civilized, it is christianized, it is rich, it is scientific; but this change is not amelioration. For everything that is given something is taken. Society acquires new arts and loses old instincts. What a contrast between the well-clad, reading, writing, thinking American, with a watch, a pencil and a bill of exchange in his pocket, and the naked New Zealander, whose property is a club, a spear, a mat and an undivided twentieth of a shed to sleep under! But compare the health of the two men and you shall see that the white man has lost his aboriginal strength. If the traveller tell us truly, strike the savage with a broad axe and in a day or two the flesh shall unite and heal as if you struck the blow into soft pitch, and the same blow shall send the white to his grave.

The civilized man has built a coach, but has lost the use of his feet. He is supported on crutches, but lacks so much support of muscle. He has a fine Geneva watch, but he fails of the skill to tell the hour by the sun. A Greenwich nautical almanac he has, and so being sure of the information when he wants it, the man in the street does not know a star in the sky. The solstice he does not observe; the equinox he knows as little; and the whole bright calendar of the year is without a dial in his mind. His note-books impair his memory; his libraries overload his wit; the insurance-office increases the number of accidents; and it may be a question whether machinery does not encumber; whether we have not lost by refinement some energy, by a Christianity, entrenched in establishments and forms, some vigor of wild virtue. For every Stoic was a Stoic; but in Christendom where is the Christian?

*

And so the reliance on Property, including the reliance on governments which protect it, is the want of self-reliance. Men have looked away from themselves and at things so long that they have come to esteem the religious, learned and civil institutions as guards of property, and they deprecate assaults on these, because they feel them to be assaults on property. They measure their esteem of each other by what each has, and not by what each is. But a cultivated man becomes ashamed of his property, out of new respect for his nature. Especially he hates what he has if he see that it is accidental, — came to him by inheritance, or gift, or crime; then he feels that it is not having; it does not belong to him, has no root in him and merely lies there because no revolution or no robber takes it away. But that which a man is, does always by necessity acquire; and what the man acquires, is living property, which does not wait the beck of rulers, or mobs, or revolutions, or fire, or storm or bankruptcies, but perpetually renews itself wherever the man breathes.

Walt Whitman: "O Living Always — Always Dying"

Emerson and Thoreau emphasize that one should not invest one's life forces in external possessions or structures, but that the secret of living consists in the act of living itself, in alive activity and awareness. This also includes the more subtle recommendation to not invest one's living self in any particular state of oneself. (Emerson's advice to not fear contradicting what one might have said earlier is an example.) One may be one kind of person at one point in one's life, and another kind of person later on, and one's views may change considerably. As an alive person I should not have any trouble leaving my former selves and opinions behind in the same way in which a snake leaves behind his old skin. To become stuck in a form of self which is not alive anymore may mean a spiritual (and sometimes more than spiritual) death. Emerson's and Thoreau's critique of the mainstream of Western culture consists, in effect, of the charge that most people die just such a premature death; that they are victims of arrested growth.

Whitman's poem (published 1860) takes up the Heraclitean thought of Emerson and Thoreau. Thus, the "dying" in his text is a sign of life, the capability of leaving behind what is past, and venturing into new forms of existence. Only those who can die are really alive. And those who are afraid to die will die, or are already dead.

O Living always — always dying!
O the burials of me, past and present!
O me, while I stride ahead, material, visible, imperious as ever!
O me, what I was for years, now dead. (I lament not — I am content);
O to disengage myself from those corpses of me, which I turn and look at, where I cast them!
To pass on, (O living! always living!) and leave the corpses behind!

Friedrich Nietzsche: "Ecce Homo"

Nietzsche's poem (published 1886; the Latin title means: "See, What a Man"—the words once used in reference to Jesus) has much the same message as Whitman's "O Living Always—Always Dying," but while Whitman used the metaphor of dying, Nietzsche uses the image of the self-consuming fire. The poem is directed against an attitude of fearful self-preservation. Nietzsche counters this attitude by suggesting a form of life which always transforms static mass (possessions, treasures, products, objects) into kinetic energy (experiences). His aim is an intensive experience of life, even if it is hard, rather than the security and inertia of an existence buttressed by accumulated material and intellectual properties. A short life of emotional and intellectual extremes is preferable to a long, but mediocre one.

Yes, I know from where I come!
Insatiable like the fire
Do I glow, consume myself.
Light is everything that I seize,
Ashes everything that I leave:
Fire am I without fail.

Johann W. Goethe: "Blissful Yearning"

Goethe's poem (published 1806; newly translated by Robert Kramer) is still another variation on the same theme—using as its central metaphor the death of the moth in the candle flame. Usually this image is used as a warning against foolish self-destruction. Goethe is aware of this common interpretation; he offers his differing conception as an *alternative for a minority of wise individuals. The point of this wisdom is the same as that of Whitman's and Nietzsche's poems: In order to live one has to die to one's old selves. The "crowd" will jeer and resist such a suggestion; they will opt for the old, known and secure. The wise, by contrast, will follow the attraction of the dangerous light and die—and thereby live again.*

Tell it to no one except the wise,
for the crowd will jeer and call you names:
The creature I most highly praise
is he who yearns for death in flames.

In the cool of night, where Eros calls you,
where you were conceived, where you begot,
a strange sensation soon befalls you
as the candle burns so still and hot.

No longer captive must you stay
within the dark of shadows waiting,
for new desire sweeps you away
and onward to a higher mating.

Now you draw near in spellbound flight,
though long you fare, you do not tire;
and finally, longing for the light,
you, moth, are all consumed in fire.

Until you know that this is best:
die—to find rebirth,
you will be but a gloomy guest
upon this darkening earth.

Arthur Rimbaud: "The Drunken Ship"

A different kind of variation of the theme of the self as flux is presented in the poem by Rimbaud (1854-1891). Rimbaud wrote the poem when he was seventeen, and suffering severely from the repressive and stifling atmosphere of the small town in Northern France where he grew up. The poem begins with visions of a ship which escapes the confines of commerce and civilization. But the visions widen into the joyful destruction of the ship itself by the boundless elements of ocean, winds, and exotic continents. The visions invoke the ecstatic return of an isolated, impoverished being to a rich and all-embracing universe—far from the deadening narrowness of European civilization.

It is clear that the ship represents the self, and the fate of the ship a longing for a form of life which is not tied to any of the roles which Western Culture offers. The forms the self can take in this civilization are all forms of alienation; the real living self will not be at home in any of them. Hence the envisioned dissolution of all forms, and the directionless drifting in the limitless elements. Self-realization here is the ecstatic dissolution of the self.

As I went down the indifferent rivers
I felt free of the guiding ropes of the haulers:
Screaming redskins had used the men as their targets,
And nailed them naked to painted stakes.

I did not care about the crew—
Haulers of Flemish wheat or English cloth.
When all this was finished, the haulers gone,
The riverflow let me drift as I wished.

I raced through furiously splashing tides—
All winter long—more stubborn than the brains of a child.

And never did severed peninsulas ever
Go under in more triumphant turmoil.

Storms gave their blessing to my maritime wakings,
I danced on the water lighter than cork,
Ten nights, called the eternal rollers of victims,
Without caring about the dull eye of the lighthouse . . .

Sweeter than a tart apple is to a child
Green water washed through my hull of pine,
Washing away the stains of blue wine
And vomit, and tearing rudder and anchor away.

And from then on I bathed in the poem
Of oceans, churning, and infused by the light of the stars,
Devouring sky-blue greens, where, delighted and pale,
At times a pensively looking dead man descends;

Where, suddenly tinting the blue, deliria
And slow rhythms under the stroking light of day,
Stronger than drink, and vaster than your music,
The bitter reds of love ferment!

I know the skies, bursting with flashes, and the gushing
And the surfs and the currents; the evening I know,
And the dawn as glittering as a swarm of doves,
And sometimes I've seen what people think they saw.

I have seen the low sun, stained with mystic horrors,
Illuminated with long, purple clots,
Resembling actors of ancient plays,
The waves that roll far off their flickering blinds.

I have dreamed the green nights of dazzling snows,
The kisses, mounting slowly to the eyes of the sea,
The circulation of unheard-of saps,
And the waking, yellow and blue, of phosphorus singing.

Whole months I followed, like stampeding cattle,
The swells in their assault on the reefs,
Not knowing that the glowing feet of the Marys
Could force the puffing snout of the seas.

I found, you know, incredible Floridas:
Panthers in human skins, their eyes among the flowers,
And rainbows stretched like bridle reins
To blue-green herds under the sea's horizon.

I saw enormous swamps ferment, and traps
With a whole Leviathan rotting in the reeds!
And falling waters in quiet zones,
And distances crashing into the abyss.

Glaciers, suns of silver, waves of pearls, embroidered skies!
Ugly debris at the end of brown gulfs,
Here giant serpents, devoured by insects,
Fall from gnarled trees with dark scents.

I would have liked to show the children these Dorados
Of the blue wave, the fish of gold, the singing fish
—Flower foams rocked by drifting, and
Indescribable winds have winged me at times.

And at times I was like a martyr, tired of poles and zones,
And the sea, whose sobbing made gentle my rolling,
Brought up her shadowy flowers, studded with bright-yellow suckers.
And so I remained, on my knees, like a woman...

Almost an island, rocking on my railings the fights
And the shit of noisy, yellow-eyed birds.
And on I rolled, while through my rotten ropes
The drowned sank backward to their sleep.

Now I, lost ship in the hair of the reefs,
Thrown by storms into birdless skies,
I, whom neither men-of-war nor Hansa ships
Could rescue, water-drunk carcass that I am,

Free, letting out smoke and purple fogs,
I, crashing through the reddening wall of the sky,
Which is covered — delicious jam for good poets! —
With lichens of sunlight and azure slime,

I, who ran, stained with electric moons,
Like a crazy plank (seahorses, black ones, go with me),
While Julys were clubbing the ultramarine
Skies of funnels ablaze,

I, who trembled, hearing at fifty leagues off
The horny groan of thick Maelstroms Behemoths,
I, the homeless roamer of azure immobilities,
I do miss Europe's ancient, narrow walls!

I've seen sidereal archipelagos! And islands,
Whose toxic skies are open to the traveller:
Is it in these boundless nights, in which you sleep,
O future power – exiled, like countless golden birds?

I've tried too long. The dawns do break my heart,
The sun is bitter, and the moon is an atrocity.
Acrid love has swollen me with drunken stupors.
I wish my keel would burst, and I would vanish in the sea!

If I desired any European water, it would be the puddle,
Cold and black, where in the fragrance-loaded dusk
A squatting, melancholy child lets go
A boat as fragile as a butterfly in May.

No longer can I, bathed in your gentle languor, waves,
Follow the routes of carriers of merchandise,
Nor go for boasting flags and fireworks,
Nor navigate beneath the evil eyes of pontoon bridges.

ILLUSTRATION NOTES

Self Determination

1. Nature and Geometry

Landscape architecture of the seventeenth century was dominated by the so-called "French Garden." This style of garden was characterized by geometrical patterns which were superimposed on nature—thus subjugating the anarchical natural growth to the disciplined regularity of the human spirit.

The following architectural period saw the development of the so-called "English Garden"—a Romantic reaction to the mathematical regularity of the French Garden. The English Garden, although by no means a wilderness, emphasized irregularity, surprise and a "natural" variety of forms.

It is evident that the French Garden corresponds to the self-conception of philosophers like Descartes, while the English Garden corresponds to that of thinkers such as Emerson.

2. Prometheus

The Torture of Prometheus, by Gustave Moreau, depicts Prometheus, the figure of Greek Mythology who was best known for stealing fire from the gods to give to man (thus making an independent human civilization possible), and for being punished for this deed by Zeus, who had him chained to a rock in the Caucasus. There the eagles of Zeus would visit him daily to eat his liver, which then regenerated prior to their next foray. According to a later legend, Prometheus was also the creator of mankind.

In the period of the Enlightenment, Prometheus became the symbol of human independence and self-reliance.

3. Nature and Technology

The engraving shows a transitional stage of the development of the external world from wilderness to total civilization. The degree of the technical transformation of reality indicates the degree to which humanity has become independent of nature (the idea expressed by the myth of Prometheus), and, according to philosophers like Fichte, how far people have progressed toward self-determination and self-realization.

4. Marx As Prometheus

This cartoon from the eighteen forties shows Marx as Prometheus, chained to a printing press, visited by the Prussian State eagle (the official emblem of the Prussian Monarchy) who is eating his liver. The cartoon satirizes the censorship problems that Marx, as newspaper editor, had been having with the state officials.

5. Man as Machine

This picture shows man analyzed as a means of production, as a quasi-work animal. As humanity became increasingly interested in harnessing nature for its purposes, humans could not help looking at themselves in the same way. Humanity as a whole can and does exploit people as another natural resource. To some philosophers this seemed to be progress toward human self-realization; to others it seemed more like self-alienation.

6. Man-made World

These three pictures show San Francisco in 1848, 1858 and at the end of the nineteenth century. They illustrate the speed with which the natural world is being replaced by civilization.

Philosophers are divided over the question of whether this man-made world is an expression of human autonomy, or the environment of complete alienation and self-loss.

7. Body and Mind

This sixteenth century engraving by Lucas van Leyden depicts a popular theme of the time: the philosopher Aristotle ridden like a horse by his mistress Phyllis. In the Western tradition up until the end of the Middle Ages, Aristotle was considered to be the greatest of thinkers, as the philosopher who had laid down all the basic categories in which people thought about themselves and their roles in life. His political writings taught that some human beings are born slaves, and that women were naturally inferior to men. He was a symbol of the rule of the male spirit over nature, which he conceived of as female and, therefore, passive. Yet, rumor had it that in his private life he had been sexually dependent on his mistress, to whom he was bound like a slave.

The engraving is also an ironic comment on Nietzsche's notorious dictum: "If you go to a woman, don't forget your whip."

8. Looking Beyond the Known World

This sixteenth century engraving depicts in a naive way the age of modernity: the confines of the traditional world with its self-conceptions have become too narrow; humanity has to look beyond these boundaries into new worlds. The outlook is frightening, for the new spaces are wide and cold, entirely lacking the metaphysical coziness and security of familiar things which furnished mankind's past existence.

About the Author

Jorn K. Bramann is Associate Professor of Philosophy at Frostburg State College, Frostburg, Maryland. He has his undergraduate degree in Philosophy and Literature from the University of Cologne, Germany, and received his PhD in Philosophy from the University of Oregon. He has taught both in the United States and in Europe. His graduate training was in Analytic Philosophy, and he has published literary as well as philosophical articles and travelled extensively in Central America, where he has studied and filmed matters pertaining to the civilization of the Maya. Dr. Bramann is editor of *Nightsun*, an annual publication emphasizing an interdisciplinary approach to both literature and philosophy. He is currently working on a book on Wittgenstein's *Tractatus Logico-Philosophicus* and Modern Art.

NOTES

Notes

NOTES

Notes

THE PEACEABLE KINGDOM

POEMS

BY

PETER WILD

"Peter Wild *makes* you come with him. The journey is exciting, a panorama of change and modulation. The quotidian is shadowed by the unusual; the daily is haunted by the mythic and magical. There is no escaping the grip. Movement, energy, an abundance almost squandered. The clauses pile up; we climb with them. And under the virtuosity, the bravura, the comedy, a kind of sadness; a grasp of the way our lives are led. Peter Wild is one of our best poets. This is a rich book."

Brian Swann

Adler Publishing Company
P.O. Box 9342
Rochester, New York
14604